Instant Vortex Plu

Fryer Oven Cookbook

For Beginners

1500 Days Healthy,Affordable and Fast Instant Vortex Plus Air Fryer Oven Recipes | 2023 Edition

Helen Mahn

CONTENTS

Breakfast Recipes

Classic Indian Malpua

Servings: 5
Cooking Time: 15 Minutes
Ingredients:

- 2 teaspoons ghee
- 1 cup all-purpose flour
- 1 cup semolina flour
- 2 cups milk
- A pinch of sea salt
- Sambal for garnish (optional)

Directions:

1. Grease a baking pan with melted ghee and set it aside.
2. In a mixing bowl, thoroughly combine the dry ingredients. In another bowl, whisk the wet ingredients. Add the wet mixture to the dry ingredients; mix to combine well.
3. Now, spoon the batter onto the prepared pan. Gently shake the pan to make sure that the batter is evenly spread.
4. Select the "Air Fry" function and adjust the temperature to 350 degrees F. Press the "Start" key. When the display indicates "Add Food", place the baking pan on the air fryer tray.
5. Cook your malpua for about 13 minutes. Cut the malpua into equal squares and serve warm with sambal, if desired. Enjoy!

Nutrition:

- Info284 Calories,5.3g Fat,48g Carbs,9.9g Protei.

Sweet Corn Muffins

Servings: 6
Cooking Time: 15 Minutes
Ingredients:

- 1 cup flour
- 1 cup yellow cornmeal
- 1/2 teaspoon salt
- 1 teaspoon baking powder
- 1 teaspoon baking soda
- 1 cup buttermilk
- 1/4 cup water
- 2 large eggs
- 1/2 cup brown sugar
- 1/4 cup butter, melted

Directions:

1. Select the "Bake" function and adjust the temperature to 330 degrees F. Press the "Start" key.
2. In a mixing bowl, stir together the dry ingredients. Then, in a separate bowl, thoroughly combine all the wet ingredients.
3. Add the wet mixture to the dry ingredients and stir just until moistened. Spoon the batter into a parchment-lined muffin tin.
4. Bake your muffins for 13 minutes or until a tester comes out dry.
5. Bon appétit!

Nutrition:

- Info315 Calories,10.2g Fat,47g Carbs,7.6g Protei.

Mexican-style Quiche

Servings: 3
Cooking Time: 20 Minutes

Ingredients:

- 1 tablespoon butter, melted
- 5 eggs
- 2 bell peppers, seeded and diced
- 1 habanero pepper, seeded and chopped
- 1 cup baby spinach leaves, roughly chopped
- 1 cup Mexican cheese blend, grated
- 1 tablespoon Mexican oregano
- Sea salt and ground black pepper, to taste

Directions:

1. Select the "Air Fry" function and adjust the temperature to 330 degrees F. Press the "Start" key.
2. Grease a baking pan with melted butter and set it aside.
3. In a mixing bowl, thoroughly combine all the ingredients. Pour the mixture into the prepared baking pan.
4. Bake your frittata for 15 minutes or until a tester comes out dry and clean.
5. Bon appétit!

Nutrition:

- Info314 Calories,21.3g Fat,9.1g Carbs,21.2g Protei.

Classic Breakfast Cups With Pesto

Servings: 2
Cooking Time: 20 Minutes

Ingredients:

- 4 eggs
- 2 ounces ham, diced
- 2 tablespoons yellow onion, chopped
- A few dashes of hot sauce
- 1 tablespoon pesto sauce
- Sea salt and ground black pepper, to taste
- 1/2 teaspoon garlic powder
- 2 ounces feta cheese, crumbled

Directions:

1. Select the "Bake" function and adjust the temperature to 350 degrees F. Press the "Start" key.
2. Line a cupcake tin with parchment paper. Mix all the ingredients until well combined. Divide the mixture between muffin cups.
3. When the display indicates "Add Food", place the muffin tin on the cooking tray.
4. Bake the breakfast cups in the preheated air fryer oven for 15 minutes. Bon appétit!

Nutrition:

- Info252 Calories,15.4g Fat,6.3g Carbs,20.7g Protei.

Chocolate Orange Muffins

Servings: 6
Cooking Time: 25 Minutes

Ingredients:

- 1 cup all-purpose flour
- 1 cup coconut flakes
- 1 teaspoon baking powder
- 1/2 teaspoon salt
- 1/2 cup chocolate chips
- 2 eggs
- 1/2 cup brown sugar
- 1/2 cup milk
- 1/2 cup orange juice
- 1 teaspoon coconut extract
- 1/4 cup coconut oil

Directions:

1. Select the "Bake" function and adjust the temperature to 330 degrees F. Press the "Start" key.
2. In a mixing bowl, stir together the dry ingredients. Then, in a separate bowl, thoroughly combine all the wet ingredients.
3. Add the wet mixture to the dry ingredients and stir just until moistened. Spoon the batter into a parchment-lined muffin tin.
4. Bake your muffins for 20 minutes or until a tester comes out dry. Enjoy!

Nutrition:

- Info365 Calories,15.5g Fat,51.3g Carbs,5.7g Protei.

Bacon And Cheese Toasted Sandwich

Servings: 1
Cooking Time: 10 Minutes

Ingredients:

- 2 slices bread
- 1 slice cheese
- 1 slice bacon

Directions:

1. Select the "Air Fry" function and adjust the temperature to 390 degrees F. Press the "Start" key. Place the bacon on the air fryer tray.
2. Air fry the bacon for 3 minutes, shaking the pan. Place the fried bacon on a paper towel and reserve.
3. Assemble your sandwich with the cheese and reserved bacon; you can use a toothpick to keep the sandwich together.
4. Select the "Toast" function and press the "Start" key.
5. Toast the sandwich for about 3 minutes or until crispy and golden brown on top; serve immediately.

Nutrition:

- Info301 Calories,18.2g Fat,22.5g Carbs,11.5g Protei.

Favorite Pizza Sandwich

Servings: 2
Cooking Time: 10 Minutes

Ingredients:

- 4 slices bread
- 2 tablespoons tomato paste
- 4 slices mozzarella cheese
- 16 slices pepperoni

Directions:

1. Assemble two sandwiches with the bread slices, tomato paste, cheese, and pepperoni; you can use a toothpick to keep the sandwich together.
2. Select the "Toast" function and press the "Start" key.
3. When the display indicates "Add Food", place the sandwich on the air fryer tray.
4. Toast the sandwich for about 3 minutes or so. Bon appétit!

Nutrition:

- Info357 Calories,17.9g Fat,24.3g Carbs,23.3g Protei.

Spinach And Feta Baked Eggs

Servings: 2
Cooking Time: 15 Minutes

Ingredients:

- 2 teaspoons olive oil
- 4 large eggs
- 2 ounces feta cheese, crumbled
- 2 tablespoons fresh scallions, sliced
- 2 cups fresh baby spinach, torn into pieces
- 1 teaspoon dried rosemary
- 1 teaspoon dried parsley flakes
- 1 teaspoon dried basil
- Coarse sea salt and ground black pepper, to taste

Directions:

1. Select the "Bake" function and adjust the temperature to 350 degrees F and the time to 13 minutes. Press the "Start" key.
2. Meanwhile, brush two ramekins with olive oil. Then crack two eggs into each ramekin. Add in the remaining ingredients.
3. When the display indicates "Add Food", place the ramekins on the cooking tray in the center position.
4. Cook the eggs until set and serve warm. Enjoy!

Nutrition:

- Info277 Calories,20.2g Fat,5.8g Carbs,18.2g Protei.

Easy Bacon Cups

Servings: 4
Cooking Time: 20 Minutes

Ingredients:

- 4 slices smoked bacon, sliced in half
- 4 thin slices tomato
- 4 eggs
- Sea salt and ground black pepper, to taste

Directions:

1. Select the "Air Fry" function and adjust the temperature to 370 degrees F. Press the "Start" key.
2. Put one slice of bacon and one slice of tomato in each muffin cup. Crack one egg on top of the tomato.
3. Sprinkle with sea salt and ground black pepper.
4. Bake in the preheated air fryer Oven for about 18 minutes. Bon appétit!

Nutrition:

- Info177 Calories,14.4g Fat,1.2g Carbs,8.9g Protei.

Aromatic Baked Eggs

Servings: 2
Cooking Time: 15 Minutes

Ingredients:

- 4 eggs
- 2 teaspoons olive oil
- 1 teaspoon rosemary
- 1 teaspoon basil
- 1/2 teaspoon garlic powder
- Sea salt and ground black pepper, to taste

Directions:

1. Select the "Bake" function and adjust the temperature to 350 degrees F and the time to 13 minutes. Press the "Start" key.
2. Meanwhile, brush two ramekins with olive oil. Then crack two eggs into each ramekin. Season the eggs with rosemary, basil, garlic, powder, salt, and pepper.
3. When the display indicates "Add Food", place the ramekins on the cooking tray in the center position.
4. Cook the eggs until set and serve warm. Enjoy!

Nutrition:

- Info169 Calories,12g Fat,1.2g Carbs,11.2g Protei.

Cheesy Egg Cups

Servings: 2
Cooking Time: 15 Minutes

Ingredients:

- 2 teaspoons olive oil
- 2 large egg
- 2 tablespoons sour cream
- 2 tablespoons cheddar cheese, grated
- Sea salt and ground black pepper, to taste

Directions:

1. Select the "Bake" function and adjust the temperature to 350 degrees F and the time to 13 minutes. Press the "Start" key.
2. Meanwhile, brush two silicone muffin cups with olive oil. Mix all the ingredients until well combined. Divide the mixture between the muffin cups.
3. When the display indicates "Add Food", place the muffin cups on the cooking tray in the center position.
4. Cook the egg cups to your desired texture, and serve warm. Enjoy!

Nutrition:

- Info277 Calories,20.2g Fat,5.8g Carbs,18.2g Protei.

Traditional Greek Tiganites

Servings: 5
Cooking Time: 15 Minutes

Ingredients:

- 1 ½ cups all-purpose flour
- 1 teaspoon baking powder
- 1/2 baking soda
- 1/2 teaspoon kosher salt
- 1 teaspoon granulated sugar
- 1 cup lukewarm water
- 1/2 cup Greek-style yogurt
- 1 large egg, whisked
- Topping:
- 1/2 cup honey

Directions:

1. In a mixing bowl, thoroughly combine the dry ingredients. In another bowl, whisk the wet ingredients. Add the wet mixture to the dry ingredients, and mix to combine well.
2. Grease a baking pan with nonstick cooking oil and set it aside.
3. Select the "Air Fry" function and adjust the temperature to 350 degrees F. Press the "Start" key.
4. Cook your tiganites for about 13 minutes or until they turn golden brown; work in batches, if needed. Enjoy!

Nutrition:

- Info222 Calories,1.3g Fat,47.3g Carbs,5.2g Protei.

Naan Pizza With Bacon

Servings: 1

Cooking Time: 10 Minutes

Ingredients:

- 1 mini naan
- 3 tablespoons marinara sauce
- 3 tablespoons Mozzarella cheese, shredded
- 1 slices bacon, diced

Directions:

1. Select the “Air Fry” function and adjust the temperature to 390 degrees F. Press the “Start” key.
2. Then, grease the cooking tray with olive oil.
3. Top your naan with marinara sauce, cheese, and bacon.
4. Bake the naan pizza for about 5 minutes or until the cheese is melted. Bon appétit!

Nutrition:

- Info525 Calories,26.1g Fat,53.3g Carbs,20.4g Protei.

Classic Breakfast Frittata

Servings: 4

Cooking Time: 20 Minutes

Ingredients:

- 1 tablespoon olive oil
- 6 eggs
- 1 shallot, peeled and chopped
- 6 tablespoons sour cream
- 1 cup Monetary-Jack cheese, shredded
- 1/2 teaspoon cayenne pepper
- Coarse sea salt and ground black pepper, to taste

Directions:

1. Select the “Air Fry” function and adjust the temperature to 330 degrees F. Press the “Start” key.
2. Grease a baking pan with nonstick cooking oil and set it aside.
3. In a mixing bowl, thoroughly combine all the ingredients. Pour the mixture into the prepared baking pan.
4. Bake your frittata for 15 minutes or until a tester comes out dry and clean.
5. Bon appétit!

Nutrition:

- Info265 Calories,20.5g Fat,3.8g Carbs,16.1g Protei.

Mustard Cheese Sandwich

Servings: 2

Cooking Time: 10 Minutes

Ingredients:

- 4 large slices crusty bread
- 2 teaspoons Dijon mustard
- 4 ounces Colby cheese, thinly sliced
- 2 tablespoons chives, roughly chopped

Directions:

1. Assemble your sandwich with mustard, cheese, and chives; you can use a toothpick to keep the sandwich together.
2. Select the "Toast" function and press the "Start" key.
3. When the display indicates "Add Food", place the sandwich on the air fryer tray.
4. Toast the sandwich for about 3 minutes. Serve immediately.

Nutrition:

- Info385 Calories,20.4g Fat,31.5g Carbs,19.1g Protei.

Breakfast Buttermilk Biscuits

Servings: 4

Cooking Time: 10 Minutes

Ingredients:

- 8 ounces refrigerated buttermilk biscuits
- 2 teaspoons mustard
- 4 slices bacon, diced
- 4 ounces cheddar cheese, cut into ten 3/4-inch cubes
- 1 tablespoon butter, melted

Directions:

1. Select the "Air Fry" function and adjust the temperature to 350 degrees F. Press the "Start" key.
2. Meanwhile, separate the dough into 4 biscuits.
3. Then, separate each biscuit into 2 layers and press them into rounds.
4. Top them with mustard, bacon, and cheese. Gently stretch the biscuit over the filling, pressing and firmly sealing around the edges of the biscuit. Brush the biscuits with melted butter.
5. When the display indicates "Add Food", place the biscuits on a parchment-lined baking tray. Bake your biscuits for about 7 minutes.
6. Bon appétit!

Nutrition:

- Info367 Calories,22.1g Fat,31.2g Carbs,11.2g Protei.

Breakfast Muffins With Almonds

Servings: 6
Cooking Time: 25 Minutes

Ingredients:

- 1/2 cup almond flour
- 1 cup all-purpose flour
- 3/4 cup granulated sugar
- 1 teaspoon baking powder
- A pinch of ground nutmeg
- A pinch of sea salt
- 1/2 teaspoon ground cinnamon
- 2 eggs, whisked
- 1/2 cup full-fat milk
- 1/4 cup butter, at room temperature
- 1/2 cup almonds, slivered

Directions:

1. Select the "Bake" function and adjust the temperature to 330 degrees F. Press the "Start" key.
2. In a mixing bowl, stir together the dry ingredients. Then, in a separate bowl, thoroughly combine all the wet ingredients.
3. Add the wet mixture to the dry ingredients and stir just until moistened.
4. Gently fold in the almonds. Spoon the batter into a parchment-lined muffin tin.
5. Bake your muffins for 20 minutes or until a tester comes out dry. Enjoy!

Nutrition:

- Info334 Calories,14.2g Fat,46g Carbs,6.7g Protei.

Vegetable And Sausage Frittata

Servings: 4
Cooking Time: 20 Minutes

Ingredients:

- 1 teaspoon olive oil
- 1/2 pound cooked breakfast sausage, crumbled
- 6 eggs, beaten
- 1/2 cup cheddar cheese, shredded
- 1 chili pepper, seeded and chopped
- 1 small red onion, chopped
- 1 teaspoon garlic, pressed
- Sea salt and ground black pepper, to taste
- 1 teaspoon paprika

Directions:

1. Select the "Air Fry" function and adjust the temperature to 330 degrees F. Press the "Start" key.
2. Grease a baking pan with olive oil and set it aside.
3. In a mixing bowl, thoroughly combine all the ingredients. Pour the mixture into the prepared baking pan.
4. Bake your frittata for 15 minutes or until a tester comes out dry and clean.
5. Bon appétit!

Nutrition:

- Info367 Calories,28.6g Fat,6.4g Carbs,19.1g Protei.

Biscuits With Smoked Sausage

Servings: 4

Cooking Time: 15 Minutes

Ingredients:

- 8 ounces refrigerated crescent dinner rolls
- 1/2 pound smoked sausage, chopped
- 1 cups cheddar cheese, shredded

Directions:

1. Select the "Air Fry" function and adjust the temperature to 350 degrees F. Press the "Start" key.
2. Meanwhile, separate the dough into 4 biscuits.
3. Unroll the crescent dough on a work surface and cut it into bite-sized pieces. Mix the crescent dough pieces with sausage and cheese. Mix to combine and roll the mixture into balls.
4. When the display indicates "Add Food", place the biscuits on a parchment-lined baking tray. Bake your biscuits for about 10 minutes.
5. Bon appétit!

Nutrition:

- Info415 Calories,23.4g Fat,32g Carbs,22.1g Protei.

Old-fashioned Donuts

Servings: 6

Cooking Time: 15 Minutes

Ingredients:

- 2 cups all-purpose flour
- 1/2 cup milk
- 2 teaspoons active dry yeast
- 2 tablespoons granulated sugar
- 1/2 teaspoon kosher salt
- 1 egg, whisked
- 1/4 cup butter, melted
- 1 cup powdered sugar

Directions:

1. Select the "Air Fry" function and adjust the temperature to 360 degrees F. Press the "Start" key.
2. Mix all the ingredients, except for the powdered sugar, until a smooth and elastic dough forms.
3. Cover your dough with plastic wrap and allow it to rise in a warm place until doubled.
4. Drop spoonfuls of the batter onto the greased baking pan. Air Fry your donuts at 360 degrees F for 15 minutes or until golden brown, flipping them halfway through the cooking time.
5. Repeat with the remaining batter. Dust warm donuts with powdered sugar. Bon appétit!

Nutrition:

- Info319 Calories,9.4g Fat,52.1g Carbs,5.9g Protei.

Vegetables And Side Dishes Recipes

Rainbow Beet Salad

Servings: 4
Cooking Time: 25 Minutes
Ingredients:

- 1 pound raw beet, peeled and cut into bite-sized pieces
- 1 teaspoon olive oil
- 2 tablespoons almonds, slivered
- 2 tablespoons pumpkin seeds, roasted
- 1 medium carrot, trimmed and julienned
- 2 cups arugula
- Vinaigrette:
- 2 tablespoons apple cider vinegar
- 1 tablespoon lime juice
- 4 tablespoons extra-virgin olive oil
- 2 tablespoons honey
- 1 teaspoon Dijon mustard
- Kosher salt and freshly cracked black pepper, to taste

Directions:

1. Toss the beets with 1 teaspoon of olive oil until well coated.
2. Select the "Air Fry" function and adjust the temperature to 400 degrees F. Press the "Start" key.
3. Arrange the beets on the air fryer oven perforated pan. Air fry the beets for 20 minutes, shaking the pan once or twice during cooking.
4. Toss the roasted beets with almonds, pumpkin seeds, carrot, and arugula. Then, in a small bowl, whisk all the vinaigrette ingredients.
5. Dress your salad and serve immediately. Enjoy!

Nutrition:

- Info281 Calories,20g Fat,23.7g Carbs,4.8g Protei.

Dilled Fried Cauliflower

Servings: 4
Cooking Time: 10 Minutes
Ingredients:

- 1 pound cauliflower florets
- 1 large egg
- 1 cup seasoned breadcrumbs
- 1 teaspoon hot paprika
- 1/2 teaspoon garlic powder
- 1 teaspoon onion powder
- 1 teaspoon dried dill weed
- Sea salt and ground black pepper, to taste
- 2 teaspoons olive oil

Directions:

1. Pat the cauliflower florets dry. Whisk the egg in a shallow bowl. In another bowl, mix the remaining ingredients.
2. Dip the cauliflower florets in the whisked egg. Then, roll the cauliflower florets into the breadcrumb mixture.
3. Select the "Air Fry" function and adjust the temperature to 380 degrees F. Press the "Start" key.
4. Arrange the cauliflower florets on the air fryer oven perforated pan, making sure not to crowd them.
5. Air fry the cauliflower florets for 9 minutes or until they're browned, shaking the pan once or twice during cooking.
6. Bon appétit!

Nutrition:

- Info188 Calories,3.8g Fat,27.8g Carbs,5.7g Protei.

Sausage-stuffed Sweet Potatoes

Servings: 4

Cooking Time: 40 Minutes

Ingredients:

- 4 medium sweet potatoes, scrubbed
- 6 ounces smoked sausage, chopped
- 4 ounces tofu cheese, chopped
- 1 medium onion, chopped
- 2 cloves garlic, minced
- 2 tablespoons fresh parsley, chopped
- 1 bell pepper, seeded and chopped
- 1 cup canned kidney beans, drained
- 1/2 cup tomato sauce
- 1 cup Colby cheese, shredded

Directions:

1. Select the "Air Fry" function and adjust the temperature to 400 degrees F. Press the "Start" key.
2. Pierce the skin of the sweet potatoes and air fry them for 15 minutes or until soft.
3. Thoroughly combine the remaining ingredients, except for the cheese, in a mixing bowl. Stuff the sweet potatoes with the prepared filling and continue baking for a further 15 minutes.
4. Select the "Broil" function. Top each potato with cheese and continue baking for 5 minutes more or until the cheese melts.
5. Bon appétit!

Nutrition:

- Info502 Calories,23.1g Fat,49.2g Carbs,25.9g Protei.

Creamed Asparagus Salad

Servings: 4

Cooking Time: 10 Minutes + Chilling Time

Ingredients:

- 1 pound asparagus, trimmed and cut into bite-sized pieces
- 1 tablespoon olive oil
- 2 cloves garlic, minced
- 1/4 cup mayonnaise
- 2 tablespoons parmesan cheese, grated
- 1 bell pepper, sliced
- 1 small red onion, sliced
- 1/2 teaspoon garlic powder
- 1 teaspoon cayenne pepper
- Kosher salt and ground black pepper, to taste

Directions:

1. Toss the asparagus with olive oil.
2. Select the "Air Fry" function and adjust the temperature to 400 degrees F. Press the "Start" key.
3. Arrange the asparagus spears on the air fryer oven perforated pan, making sure not to crowd them.
4. Air fry the asparagus for 8 minutes or until tender and bright green, tossing halfway through cooking time.
5. Toss the asparagus with the other ingredients; toss to combine well and serve at room temperature or well-chilled. Enjoy!

Nutrition:

- Info179 Calories,14.6g Fat,9.6g Carbs,4.2g Protei.

Easy Roasted Asparagus

Servings: 4
Cooking Time: 10 Minutes

Ingredients:

- 1 ½ pounds asparagus, trimmed
- 2 tablespoons olive oil
- 1 teaspoon cayenne pepper
- 1 teaspoon granulated garlic (or garlic powder)
- 1 teaspoon grated lemon zest
- Kosher salt and freshly cracked black pepper, to taste

Directions:

1. Toss all the ingredients in a mixing bowl.
2. Select the "Air Fry" function and adjust the temperature to 400 degrees F. Press the "Start" key.
3. Arrange the asparagus spears on the air fryer oven perforated pan, making sure not to crowd them.
4. Air fry the asparagus for 8 minutes or until tender and bright green, tossing halfway through the cooking time.
5. Bon appétit!

Nutrition:

- Info96 Calories,7g Fat,7.2g Carbs,3.8g Protei.

Mashed Sweet Potatoes

Servings: 4
Cooking Time: 35 Minutes

Ingredients:

- 1 ½ pounds sweet potatoes, peeled and halved
- 1 tablespoon olive oil
- 2 tablespoons butter
- 1 teaspoon red pepper flakes, crushed
- Kosher salt and ground black pepper, to taste

Directions:

1. Toss the sweet potatoes with olive oil in a mixing bowl.
2. Select the "Air Fry" function and adjust the temperature to 400 degrees F. Press the "Start" key.
3. Arrange your sweet potatoes on the parchment-lined air fryer oven perforated pan.
4. Roast your sweet potatoes for 30 minutes or until tender and cooked through. Mash the sweet potatoes with the remaining ingredients.
5. Bon appétit!

Nutrition:

- Info236 Calories,9.2g Fat,35.4g Carbs,2.9g Protei.

Buttery Green Beans

Servings: 4
Cooking Time: 15 Minutes

Ingredients:

- 1 pound fresh green beans, trimmed
- 2 teaspoons butter, melted
- Sea salt and ground black pepper, to taste
- 1 teaspoon hot paprika
- 1/2 teaspoon onion powder
- 1/2 teaspoon garlic powder

Directions:

1. Toss the green beans with the other ingredients in a mixing bowl.
2. Select the “Air Fry” function and adjust the temperature to 400 degrees F. Press the “Start” key.
3. Arrange the green beans on the parchment-lined air fryer oven perforated pan.
4. Air fry the green beans for 10 minutes or until they achieve a light brown color.
5. Bon appétit!

Nutrition:

- Info68 Calories,2.2g Fat,9.8g Carbs,2.7g Protei.

Parmesan Fennel Patties

Servings: 4
Cooking Time: 20 Minutes

Ingredients:

- 1 pound fennel, trimmed and chopped
- 1 small onion, chopped
- 2 garlic cloves, minced
- 2 eggs, whisked
- 1/2 cup parmesan cheese, grated
- 2 tablespoons chives, chopped
- 2 tablespoons parsley, chopped
- 1 teaspoon lemon zest
- Sea salt and ground black pepper, to taste
- 1 cup all-purpose flour
- 2 tablespoons olive oil

Directions:

1. Select the “Air Fry” function and adjust the temperature to 380 degrees F. Press the “Start” key.
2. Place a sheet of parchment paper in the air fryer oven pan. Thoroughly combine all the ingredients.
3. Form the mixture into four patties and place them in a single layer in the air fryer oven perforated pan.
4. Air fry the patties for 15 minutes, turning them over halfway through.
5. Bon appétit!

Nutrition:

- Info341 Calories,15.6g Fat,37.8g Carbs,13.3g Protei.

Warm Eggplant Salad

Servings: 4
Cooking Time: 20 Minutes

Ingredients:

- 1 pound eggplant
- 1 teaspoon butter, melted
- 1 medium tomato, diced
- 1 sweet onion, diced
- 1 red chili pepper, chopped
- 2 tablespoons fresh mint leaves chopped
- 1/2 teaspoon ground cumin
- 1/2 teaspoon mustard seeds
- 1 garlic clove, minced
- 2 tablespoons freshly squeezed lemon juice
- 6 tablespoons extra-virgin olive oil
- Kosher salt and ground black pepper, to taste

Directions:

1. In a mixing bowl, toss the eggplant with 1 teaspoon of melted butter.
2. Select the "Air Fry" function and adjust the temperature to 390 degrees F. Press the "Start" key.
3. Place the eggplant on the parchment-lined air fryer oven perforated pan.
4. Roast the eggplant for 10 minutes. Add in the tomato and onion and continue cooking for a further 5 minutes.
5. Toss the roasted veggies with the remaining ingredients.
6. Bon appétit!

Nutrition:

- Info258 Calories,21.7g Fat,16.2g Carbs,2.5g Protei.

Golden Dijon Potatoes

Servings: 4
Cooking Time: 40 Minutes

Ingredients:

- 1 ½ pounds potatoes, peeled and diced
- 1/2 cup mayonnaise
- Coarse sea salt and freshly ground black pepper, to season
- 1 teaspoon lemon zest
- 1 tablespoon lemon juice
- 2 cloves garlic, minced
- 1 tablespoon Dijon mustard

Directions:

1. Toss all the ingredients in a mixing bowl.
2. Select the "Roast" function and adjust the temperature to 380 degrees F. Press the "Start" key.
3. Arrange your potatoes on the parchment-lined air fryer oven perforated pan.
4. Roast your potatoes for 35 minutes or until tender and cooked through. Serve warm and enjoy!

Nutrition:

- Info324 Calories,20.8g Fat,30.9g Carbs,4g Protei.

Beet Salad With Gruyere Cheese

Servings: 4
Cooking Time: 25 Minutes

Ingredients:

- 1 pound fresh beets, peeled and cut into 1-inch pieces cubes
- 2 tablespoons extra-virgin olive oil
- 2 tablespoons red wine vinegar
- 1/2 teaspoon cumin
- 1/2 teaspoon mustard seeds
- Kosher salt and ground black pepper, to taste
- 4 ounces Gruyere cheese, crumbled

Directions:

1. Toss all the ingredients in a mixing bowl, except for the cheese.
2. Select the "Air Fry" function and adjust the temperature to 400 degrees F. Press the "Start" key.
3. Arrange the beets on the air fryer oven perforated pan, making sure not to crowd them.
4. Air fry the beets for 20 minutes or until they're browned, shaking the pan once or twice during cooking.
5. Top the roasted beets with cheese and enjoy!

Nutrition:

- Info235 Calories,16.4g Fat,12.2g Carbs,10.6g Protei.

Ritzy Stuffed Mushrooms

Servings: 4
Cooking Time: 20 Minutes

Ingredients:

- 1 pound button mushrooms, stalks removed
- 1/2 cup crackers, crushed
- 2 cloves garlic, minced
- 2 tablespoons butter, softened
- Kosher salt and freshly ground black pepper, to taste
- 1/4 cup Pecorino cheese, grated
- 2 tablespoons fresh parsley, chopped
- 2 tablespoons fresh cilantro, chopped

Directions:

1. Pat the mushrooms dry. Toss the remaining ingredients in a mixing bowl.
2. Divide the filling between the prepared mushrooms.
3. Select the "Air Fry" function and adjust the temperature to 350 degrees F. Press the "Start" key.
4. Arrange the mushrooms on the parchment-lined air fryer oven perforated pan. Bake the mushrooms for 12 minutes or until tender and cooked through.
5. Bon appétit!

Nutrition:

- Info148 Calories,10.6g Fat,8.3g Carbs,6.1g Protei.

Greek-style Eggplant

Servings: 4
Cooking Time: 20 Minutes

Ingredients:

- 1 ½ pounds eggplants, diced
- 1 teaspoon garlic, minced
- 1 teaspoon dried oregano
- 1 teaspoon dried basil
- 2 tablespoons extra-virgin olive oil
- 1 teaspoon paprika
- Coarse sea salt and ground black pepper, to taste

Directions:

1. Toss all the ingredients in a mixing bowl.
2. Select the "Air Fry" function and adjust the temperature to 390 degrees F. Press the "Start" key.
3. Arrange your eggplant on the parchment-lined air fryer oven perforated pan.
4. Roast the eggplant for 15 minutes or until tender and cooked through.
5. Bon appétit!

Nutrition:

- Info111 Calories,7.2g Fat,11.8g Carbs,2.1g Protei.

Roasted Carrot Mash

Servings: 4
Cooking Time: 25 Minutes

Ingredients:

- 1 ½ pounds carrots, trimmed and sliced
- 2 tablespoons olive oil
- 2 tablespoons butter
- 1 teaspoon ground cumin
- 1/4 teaspoon dried dill weed
- Sea salt and ground black pepper, to season
- 1 teaspoon cayenne pepper
- 1/2 cup whole milk

Directions:

1. Toss the carrots with olive oil in a mixing bowl.
2. Select the "Air Fry" function and adjust the temperature to 380 degrees F. Press the "Start" key.
3. Arrange your carrots on the parchment-lined air fryer oven perforated pan.
4. Air fry your carrots for 20 minutes or until tender and cooked through. Mash the carrots with the remaining ingredients until creamy and uniform.
5. Bon appétit!

Nutrition:

- Info219 Calories,14.1g Fat,21.8g Carbs,2.9g Protei.

Cheese-stuffed Mushrooms

Servings: 4
Cooking Time: 15 Minutes

Ingredients:

- 12 button mushrooms, washed
- 1 tablespoon olive oil
- 2 garlic cloves, minced
- 1/2 cup Parmesan cheese, grated
- 4 tablespoons tortilla chips, crushed
- Sea salt and ground black pepper, to taste
- 1/2 teaspoon mustard powder
- 1/2 teaspoon onion powder

Directions:

1. Pat the mushrooms dry and remove the stalks.
2. In a mixing bowl, thoroughly combine the remaining ingredients. Divide the filling between the prepared mushrooms.
3. Select the "Air Fry" function and adjust the temperature to 360 degrees F. Press the "Start" key.
4. Arrange the mushrooms on the air fryer oven perforated pan, making sure not to crowd them.
5. Air fry the mushrooms for 9 minutes or until cooked through.
6. Bon appétit!

Nutrition:

- Info239 Calories,9.8g Fat,29.4g Carbs,9.3g Protei.

Blue Cheese Cauliflower

Servings: 4
Cooking Time: 10 Minutes

Ingredients:

- 1 pound cauliflower florets
- 1 tablespoon olive oil
- 1/2 teaspoon ground turmeric
- 1/2 teaspoon smoked paprika
- 1 teaspoon fennel seeds
- Sea salt and ground black pepper, to taste
- 4 tablespoons blue cheese, crumbled

Directions:

1. Toss all the ingredients in a mixing bowl.
2. Select the "Air Fry" function and adjust the temperature to 380 degrees F. Press the "Start" key.
3. Arrange the cauliflower florets on the air fryer oven perforated pan, making sure not to crowd them.
4. Air fry the cauliflower florets for 9 minutes or until they're browned, shaking the pan once or twice during cooking.
5. Bon appétit!

Nutrition:

- Info105 Calories,5.2g Fat,8g Carbs,3.9g Protei.

Cheesy Roasted Parsnips

Servings: 4
Cooking Time: 25 Minutes

Ingredients:

- 1 ½ pounds parsnips, sliced into 1/2-inch chunks
- 4 tablespoons butter
- 4 cloves garlic, pressed
- Kosher salt and freshly ground black pepper, to taste
- 1 teaspoon red pepper flakes, crushed
- 4 ounces cheddar cheese, grated

Directions:

1. Toss the parsnip, butter, garlic, and spices in a mixing bowl.
2. Select the "Air Fry" function and adjust the temperature to 380 degrees F. Press the "Start" key.
3. Arrange your parsnip on the parchment-lined air fryer oven perforated pan.
4. Air fry your parsnip for 15 minutes or until tender and cooked through. Top the parsnips with cheese and select the "Broil" function.
5. Continue baking for a further 5 minutes or until the cheese melts and browns slightly. Serve warm and enjoy!

Nutrition:

- Info349 Calories,21.6g Fat,32.1g Carbs,9.2g Protei.

Traditional Greek Marathokeftedes

Servings: 4
Cooking Time: 15 Minutes

Ingredients:

- 1 pound fennel bulbs, trimmed and chopped
- 4 spring onions, finely chopped
- 1 teaspoon dried Greek oregano
- 2 tablespoons fresh mint leaves, chopped
- 2 tablespoons fresh parsley leaves, chopped
- 1 cup all-purpose flour
- 1/2 cup feta cheese, crumbled
- 2 tablespoons olive oil

Directions:

1. Select the "Air Fry" function and adjust the temperature to 380 degrees F. Press the "Start" key.
2. Place a sheet of parchment paper in the air fryer oven pan. Thoroughly combine all the ingredients.
3. Form the mixture into equal balls and place them in a single layer in the air fryer oven perforated pan.
4. Air fry the Greek marathokeftedes for 13 minutes, turning them over halfway through.
5. Bon appétit!

Nutrition:

- Info266 Calories,11.4g Fat,34.4g Carbs,7.7g Protei.

Italian-style Croquettes

Servings: 4
Cooking Time: 15 Minutes

Ingredients:

- 1 pound cauliflower, grated
- 1 small onion, chopped
- 2 garlic cloves, minced
- 2 tablespoons olive oil
- 1/2 tsp Italian seasoning
- 1 cup mozzarella cheese
- 1 large egg, beaten
- 1/2 cup all-purpose flour
- Kosher salt and ground black pepper, to taste

Directions:

1. Select the "Air Fry" function and adjust the temperature to 390 degrees F. Press the "Start" key.
2. Place a sheet of parchment paper in the air fryer oven pan. Thoroughly combine all the ingredients.
3. Form the mixture into equal balls and place them in a single layer in the air fryer oven perforated pan.
4. Air fry the croquettes for 10 minutes, turning them over halfway through.
5. Bon appétit!

Nutrition:

- Info212 Calories,8.4g Fat,20.9g Carbs,14.8g Protei.

Smoked Cauliflower Bites

Servings: 4
Cooking Time: 10 Minutes

Ingredients:

- 1 pound cauliflower florets
- 2 tablespoons butter, at room temperature
- 2 cloves garlic, crushed
- 1 tablespoon olive oil
- 1 teaspoon smoked paprika
- Sea salt and ground black pepper, to taste

Directions:

1. Toss all the ingredients in a mixing bowl.
2. Select the "Air Fry" function and adjust the temperature to 380 degrees F. Press the "Start" key.
3. Arrange the cauliflower florets on the air fryer oven perforated pan, making sure not to crowd them.
4. Air fry the cauliflower florets for 9 minutes or until they're browned, shaking the pan once or twice during cooking.
5. Bon appétit!

Nutrition:

- Info118 Calories,9.5g Fat,6.4g Carbs,2.7g Protei.

Vegan Recipes

Vegan Blt Sandwich

Servings: 1
Cooking Time: 35 Minutes

Ingredients:

- 2 slices eggplant
- 1/2 teaspoon smoked paprika
- 1 tablespoon olive oil
- 2 slices bread
- 2 tablespoons vegan mayo
- 1 green onion stalks, chopped
- 1/2 small ripe tomato
- 2 leaves green lettuce

Directions:

1. Select the "Air Fry" function and adjust the temperature to 380 degrees F. Press the "Start" key.
2. To make the vegan bacon, toss the eggplant slices with the smoked paprika and olive oil. Arrange the eggplant slices on the parchment-lined air fryer oven perforated pan.
3. Air fry your eggplant pieces for 25 minutes or until crispy.
4. Assemble your sandwich with the eggplant bacon and the other ingredients. You can toast your sandwich on the "Toast" function if desired.
5. Serve immediately and enjoy!

Nutrition:

- Info369 Calories,25.2g Fat,32g Carbs,5.5g Protei.

Easy Fried Tempeh

Servings: 4
Cooking Time: 25 Minutes

Ingredients:

- 12 ounces tempeh, sliced
- 1 tablespoon stone-ground mustard
- 2 tablespoons rice vinegar
- 1 teaspoon red pepper flakes
- 2 tablespoons soy sauce
- A few dashes of liquid smoke

Directions:

1. In a ceramic bowl, thoroughly combine all the ingredients. Cover and let it marinate for about 1 hour.
2. Select the "Air Fry" function and adjust the temperature to 395 degrees F. Press the "Start" key.
3. Arrange the tempeh slice on the air fryer oven perforated pan, making sure not to crowd them. Reserve the marinade.
4. Air fry the tempeh slices for 10 minutes. Flip the tempeh slices and baste them with the reserved marinade; continue to cook for 10 minutes longer or until golden brown.
5. Bon appétit!

Nutrition:

- Info197 Calories,11.2g Fat,10.5g Carbs,16.7g Protei.

Cashew Oatmeal Muffins

Servings: 8
Cooking Time: 20 Minutes

Ingredients:

- 2 cups old-fashioned rolled oats
- 1 teaspoon baking powder
- 1/2 teaspoon baking soda
- 2 cups oat milk (or cashew milk)
- 1/2 cup cashew butter
- 2 bananas, mashed
- 1/4 cup agave syrup
- 1 teaspoon pure vanilla extract
- A pinch of kosher salt and grated nutmeg
- 1 teaspoon ground cinnamon

Directions:

1. Select the "Air Fry" function and adjust the temperature to 390 degrees F. Press the "Start" key.
2. Thoroughly combine all the ingredients. Spoon the mixture into lightly greased muffin cups.
3. Air fry the oatmeal cups for 15 minutes or until golden brown.
4. Bon appétit!

Nutrition:

- Info229 Calories,15.2g Fat,27g Carbs,6.1g Protei.

Classic Lentil Meatballs

Servings: 4
Cooking Time: 20 Minutes

Ingredients:

- 2 cups red lentils, cooked and rinsed
- 1/2 cup whole-wheat flour
- 1/2 teaspoon baking powder
- 2 tablespoons walnuts, ground
- 1 tablespoon flaxseed, ground
- 2 teaspoons nutritional yeast
- 1 small onion, chopped
- 2 garlic cloves, pressed
- 1/4 cup tomato paste
- 2 tablespoons fresh parsley leaves, chopped
- 1 tablespoon fresh dill weed, chopped
- Sea salt and ground black pepper, to taste
- 1 teaspoon smoked paprika

Directions:

1. Select the "Air Fry" function and adjust the temperature to 400 degrees F. Press the "Start" key.
2. Place a sheet of parchment paper in the air fryer oven pan. Thoroughly combine all the ingredients.
3. Form the mixture into equal balls and place them in a single layer in the air fryer oven perforated pan.
4. Air fry the balls for 15 minutes or until cooked through. Serve hot and enjoy!

Nutrition:

- Info305 Calories,10.5g Fat,40.4g Carbs,17.1g Protei.

Toasted Tortillas With Avocado

Servings: 2
Cooking Time: 10 Minutes
Ingredients:

- 2 whole-wheat tortillas
- 1/3 cup hummus
- 2 tablespoons tomato ketchup
- 1/2 avocado, pitted, peeled and sliced
- Handful fresh arugula

Directions:

1. Assemble taco wraps by filling each tortilla with equal amount of the rest of the ingredients.
2. Select the "Toast" function and press the "Start" key.
3. Toast your taco wraps for 3 minutes or so.
4. Serve immediately and enjoy!

Nutrition:

- Info297 Calories,15g Fat,33.5g Carbs,7.7g Protei.

Fried Tofu With Sweet Potatoes

Servings: 5
Cooking Time: 35 Minutes
Ingredients:

- 1 pound sweet potatoes, peeled and cut into 1-inch chunks
- 10 ounces extra-firm tofu, pressed and cut into 1-inch chunks
- 1 teaspoon garlic, minced
- 2 tablespoons scallions, chopped
- 1 teaspoon paprika - divided
- Kosher salt and ground black pepper, to taste
- 2 tablespoons cornstarch
- 2 tablespoons olive oil

Directions:

1. In a mixing bowl, thoroughly combine all the ingredients.
2. Select the "Air Fry" function and adjust the temperature to 395 degrees F. Press the "Start" key.
3. Arrange the sweet potatoes on the air fryer oven perforated pan, making sure not to crowd them.
4. Air fry the sweet potatoes for 20 minutes or until soft; make sure to toss them occasionally to ensure even cooking.
5. Add in the tofu cubes and continue cooking for a further 10 minutes or until cooked through.
6. Bon appétit!

Nutrition:

- Info188 Calories,8.8g Fat,21.4g Carbs,7.7g Protei.

Breaded Avocado Wedges

Servings: 4

Cooking Time: 10 Minutes

Ingredients:

- 1/2 cup all-purpose flour
- 4 tablespoons vegan mayonnaise
- 1/4 cup cream of celery soup
- 2 garlic cloves, minced
- 1 cup breadcrumbs
- 1 teaspoon hot paprika
- Kosher salt and freshly ground black pepper, to taste
- 2 medium avocados, pitted, peeled and cut into wedges
- 2 teaspoon peanut oil (or toasted sesame oil)

Directions:

1. In a shallow bowl, mix the flour, mayonnaise, soup, and garlic. In another bowl, thoroughly combine breadcrumbs, hot paprika, salt, and black pepper.
2. Dip the avocado into the flour mixture. Then, dredge the avocado wedges in the breadcrumb mixture. Brush the avocado wedges with peanut oil on all sides.
3. When the display indicates "Add Food", place the avocado wedges in the air fryer oven perforated pan. Air fry them at 400 degrees F for 6 minutes.
4. Enjoy!

Nutrition:

- Info325 Calories,22.7g Fat,27.4g Carbs,5.8g Protei.

Smoked Tempeh Sandwich

Servings: 3

Cooking Time: 25 Minutes

Ingredients:

- 9 ounces tempeh, sliced
- 1 tablespoon Dijon mustard
- 2 tablespoons soy sauce
- 2 tablespoons red wine vinegar
- 2 tablespoons tomato paste
- 1 garlic clove, pressed
- 2 scallion stalks, chopped
- 1 teaspoon smoked paprika
- 6 slices whole-grain bread

Directions:

1. In a ceramic bowl, thoroughly combine all the ingredients, except for the bread. Cover and let it marinate for about 1 hour.
2. Select the "Air Fry" function and adjust the temperature to 395 degrees F. Press the "Start" key.
3. Arrange the tempeh slice on the air fryer oven perforated pan, making sure not to crowd them. Reserve the marinade.
4. Air fry the tempeh slices for 10 minutes. Flip the tempeh slices and baste them with the reserved marinade; continue to cook for 10 minutes longer or until golden brown.
5. Assemble your sandwiches with bread slices and roasted tempeh; serve immediately and enjoy!

Nutrition:

- Info451 Calories,15.2g Fat,53.2g Carbs,30.5g Protei.

Roasted Peppers With Tofu

Servings: 4
Cooking Time: 20 Minutes

Ingredients:

- 4 bell peppers, seeded and quartered
- 1 tablespoon olive oil
- 1 tablespoon taco seasoning mix
- Sea salt and ground black pepper, to taste
- 2 garlic cloves, minced
- 2 ounces tofu, crumbled

Directions:

1. Toss all the ingredients in a mixing bowl.
2. Select the "Air Fry" function and adjust the temperature to 400 degrees F. Press the "Start" key.
3. Toss the peppers with olive oil, spices, and garlic; place them on the air fryer oven perforated pan, making sure not to crowd them.
4. Air fry the peppers and tofu for 10 minutes or until they're browned, shaking the pan once or twice during cooking.
5. Top the peppers with tofu and select the "Broil" function; continue to cook for 5 minutes more or until cooked through.
6. Bon appétit!

Nutrition:

- Info109 Calories,4.5g Fat,14.8g Carbs,3.5g Protei.

Mediterranean-style Oatmeal Cups

Servings: 6
Cooking Time: 20 Minutes

Ingredients:

- 2 tablespoons olive oil
- 1 tablespoon coconut oil, softened
- 1 shallot, chopped
- 1 teaspoon garlic powder
- 1 teaspoon cayenne pepper
- 1 ½ cups old-fashioned rolled oats
- 3/4 cup oat milk (or rice milk)
- 1/3 cup tofu cheese, grated
- 1/4 cup sun-dried tomatoes, chopped
- 1 ounce black olives, pitted and chopped
- Sea salt and ground black pepper, to taste

Directions:

1. Select the "Air Fry" function and adjust the temperature to 390 degrees F. Press the "Start" key.
2. Thoroughly combine all the ingredients. Spoon the mixture into a greased muffin tin.
3. Air fry the oatmeal cups for 15 minutes or until golden brown.
4. Bon appétit!

Nutrition:

- Info269 Calories,12.5g Fat,3.2g Carbs,10.5g Protei.

Rosemary Roasted Potatoes

Servings: 4
Cooking Time: 40 Minutes

Ingredients:

- 1 ½ pounds potatoes, peeled and cut into quarters
- 2 tablespoons olive oil
- Coarse sea salt and freshly ground black pepper, to taste
- 1 teaspoon cayenne pepper
- 1 tablespoon dried rosemary, minced

Directions:

1. Select the "Air Fry" function and adjust the temperature to 400 degrees F. Press the "Start" key.
2. Toss the potato chunks with the remaining ingredients.
3. When the display indicates "Add Food", place the potato chunks in the air fryer oven perforated pan.
4. Air fry the potatoes for 35 minutes, turning them over at the halfway point.
5. Bon appétit!

Nutrition:

- Info193 Calories,7.1g Fat,30.1g Carbs,3.5g Protei.

Carrot Puree With Herbs

Servings: 4
Cooking Time: 25 Minutes

Ingredients:

- 1 pound carrots, trimmed and halved lengthwise
- 1 tablespoon olive oil
- 2 garlic cloves, minced
- 1/4 cup cream of celery soup
- 2 tablespoons tahini
- Sea salt and cayenne pepper, to taste
- 1 teaspoon red pepper flakes, crushed
- 1 tablespoon fresh parsley, chopped
- 1 tablespoon fresh cilantro, chopped
- 1 tablespoon fresh sage, chopped

Directions:

1. Toss the carrots with olive oil.
2. Select the "Air Fry" function and adjust the temperature to 380 degrees F. Press the "Start" key.
3. Arrange your carrots on the parchment-lined air fryer oven perforated pan.
4. Air fry your carrots for 20 minutes or until tender and cooked through.
5. Next, puree the roasted carrots with the garlic, soup, tahini, salt, and cayenne pepper until everything is well incorporated.
6. Garnish your puree with red pepper flakes and herbs. Bon appétit!

Nutrition:

- Info136 Calories,8.1g Fat,14.9g Carbs,2.9g Protei.

Classic Toasted Sandwich

Servings: 1
Cooking Time: 10 Minutes

Ingredients:

- 4 slices bread
- 2 tablespoons hummus
- 1 small tomato, sliced
- 2 lettuce leaves

Directions:

1. Assemble your sandwich with hummus, tomato, and lettuce; you can use a toothpick to keep the sandwich together.
2. When the display indicates “Add Food”, place the sandwich on the air fryer tray.
3. Select the “Toast” function and press the “Start” key.
4. Toast your sandwich for about 3 minutes or so. Serve immediately.

Nutrition:

- Info277 Calories,5.3g Fat,46.4g Carbs,8.8g Protei.

Italian-style Eggplant

Servings: 4
Cooking Time: 20 Minutes

Ingredients:

- 1 pound eggplant, sliced
- 1 teaspoon garlic powder
- 1 teaspoon onion powder
- 1 teaspoon hot paprika
- Kosher salt and ground black pepper, to taste
- 1/4 teaspoon ground cumin
- 2 tablespoons olive oil
- 1/2 cup marinara sauce

Directions:

1. In a mixing bowl, toss the eggplant with the spices and olive oil.
2. Select the “Air Fry” function and adjust the temperature to 390 degrees F. Press the “Start” key.
3. Place the eggplant on the parchment-lined air fryer oven perforated pan.
4. Roast the eggplant for 10 minutes. Top them with marinara sauce; continue to cook for a further 5 minutes.
5. Bon appétit!

Nutrition:

- Info109 Calories,7.1g Fat,11.3g Carbs,2.1g Protei.

Crispy Breaded Mushrooms

Servings: 4
Cooking Time: 15 Minutes

Ingredients:

- 1 pound brown mushrooms
- 1/4 cup oat milk (or rice milk)
- 1 cup tortilla chips, crushed
- 2 teaspoon olive oil
- 2 garlic cloves, minced
- Sea salt and ground black pepper, to taste
- 1 teaspoon smoked paprika
- 2 tablespoons nutritional yeast

Directions:

1. Pat the mushrooms dry.
2. In a mixing bowl, thoroughly combine all the remaining ingredients. Then, dip the mushrooms in the breadcrumb mixture, coating them on all sides.
3. Select the "Air Fry" function and adjust the temperature to 360 degrees F. Press the "Start" key.
4. Arrange the mushrooms on the air fryer oven perforated pan, making sure not to crowd them. Air fry the mushrooms for 10 minutes or until golden brown.
5. Bon appétit!

Nutrition:

- Info243 Calories,10.7g Fat,30.1g Carbs,8.6g Protei.

Cauliflower Tater Tots

Servings: 4
Cooking Time: 15 Minutes

Ingredients:

- 1 pound cauliflower rice
- 2 tablespoons olive oil
- 1 cup rice milk (oat milk)
- 1 cup plain flour
- 1/2 cup tahini paste
- 2 scallion stalks, chopped
- 1 cup panko breadcrumbs

Directions:

1. Select the "Air Fry" function and adjust the temperature to 390 degrees F. Press the "Start" key.
2. Place a sheet of parchment paper in the air fryer oven pan. Thoroughly combine all the ingredients.
3. Form the mixture into equal balls and place them in a single layer in the air fryer oven perforated pan.
4. Air fry the balls for 10 minutes, turning them over halfway through.
5. Bon appétit!

Nutrition:

- Info414 Calories,17.7g Fat,54.4g Carbs,12.5g Protei.

Spicy Red Potatoes

Servings: 4
Cooking Time: 40 Minutes

Ingredients:

- 1 ½ pounds red potatoes, peeled and cut into wedges
- 3 tablespoons olive oil
- 2 garlic cloves, pressed
- 1 teaspoon hot sauce
- Sea salt and ground black pepper, to taste

Directions:

1. Select the "Air Fry" function and adjust the temperature to 400 degrees F. Press the "Start" key.
2. Toss the potato wedges with the remaining ingredients.
3. When the display indicates "Add Food", place the potato wedges in the air fryer oven perforated pan.
4. Air fry the potato wedges for 35 minutes, turning them over at the halfway point.
5. Bon appétit!

Nutrition:

- Info217 Calories,10.4g Fat,28.7g Carbs,3.5g Protei.

Roasted Golden Beets

Servings: 4
Cooking Time: 25 Minutes

Ingredients:

- 1 pound golden beets, scrubbed and diced
- 1/4 cup olive oil
- 2 tablespoons apple cider vinegar
- Coarse sea salt and ground black pepper, to taste
- 1/2 teaspoon ground cumin
- 1 tablespoon Dijon mustard

Directions:

1. Toss the golden beets with 1 tablespoon of olive oil in a mixing bowl.
2. Select the "Air Fry" function and adjust the temperature to 400 degrees F. Press the "Start" key.
3. Arrange the beets on the air fryer oven perforated pan, making sure not to crowd them.
4. Air fry the beets for 20 minutes or until they're browned, shaking the pan once or twice during cooking.
5. Toss the roasted beets with the remaining ingredients and serve at room temperature.
6. Bon appétit!

Nutrition:

- Info179 Calories,13.9g Fat,12.3g Carbs,2.3g Protei.

Kid-friendly Corn Muffins

Servings: 6

Cooking Time: 15 Minutes

Ingredients:

- 1 ½ cups all-purpose flour
- 1 cup cornmeal
- 1 teaspoon baking powder
- 1/2 teaspoon baking soda
- 1/2 cup creamed corn kernels
- 1/4 cup agave syrup
- 1 teaspoon salt
- 1/4 teaspoon grated nutmeg
- 1 cup almond milk
- 1/4 cup applesauce

Directions:

1. Select the "Bake" function and adjust the temperature to 390 degrees F. Press the "Start" key.
2. In a mixing bowl, stir together the dry ingredients. Then, in a separate bowl, thoroughly combine all the wet ingredients.
3. Add the wet mixture to the dry ingredients and stir just until moistened. Spoon the batter into a parchment-lined muffin tin.
4. Bake your muffins for 5 minutes. Reduce temperature to 330 degrees F and continue to bake for a further 7 minutes or until a tester comes out dry.
5. Bon appétit!

Nutrition:

- Info294 Calories,3.3g Fat,60.4g Carbs,7.5g Protei.

Appetizers And Snacks Recipes

Baked Pita Wedges

Servings: 4
Cooking Time: 10 Minutes

Ingredients:

- 4 small pitas, cut into triangles
- 2 tablespoons extra-virgin olive oil
- 1 teaspoon garlic powder
- 1 teaspoon dried oregano
- 1 teaspoon dried rosemary
- Coarse sea salt and ground black pepper, to season

Directions:

1. Select the “Air Fry” function and adjust the temperature to 330 degrees F. Press the “Start” key.
2. Place a sheet of parchment paper in the air fryer oven pan.
3. Toss the pita triangles with the remaining ingredients. Air fry the pita triangles for 6 minutes, turning them over halfway through.
4. Bon appétit!

Nutrition:

- Info138 Calories,7.5g Fat,16.1g Carbs,2.9g Protei.

Parmesan Cocktail Meatballs

Servings: 6
Cooking Time: 20 Minutes

Ingredients:

- 1 pound ground pork
- 1/2 pound ground beef
- 1 cup breadcrumbs
- 1/4 cup milk
- 4 cloves garlic, pressed or minced
- 2 eggs, beaten
- 1 cup Parmesan cheese, grated
- 1/4 cup parsley, chopped
- 1 small onion, chopped
- 1 teaspoon dried oregano
- 1 teaspoon cayenne pepper
- Sea salt and ground black pepper, to taste

Directions:

1. Select the “Air Fry” function and adjust the temperature to 380 degrees F. Press the “Start” key.
2. Place a sheet of parchment paper in the air fryer oven pan.
3. In a mixing bowl, thoroughly combine all the ingredients. Then, drop rounds of the mixture in a single layer onto the prepared pan using a small scoop.
4. Air fry the meatballs for 10 minutes.
5. Select the “Broil” function and cook your meatballs for a further 5 minutes or until cooked through.
6. Bon appétit!

Nutrition:

- Info398 Calories,27.4g Fat,8.6g Carbs,28g Protei.

Parmesan Eggplant Chips

Servings: 7
Cooking Time: 20 Minutes

Ingredients:

- 1 pound eggplant, sliced
- 2 large eggs
- 1/2 cup Parmesan cheese, grated
- 1 clove garlic, minced
- Sea salt and ground black pepper, to taste
- 1 teaspoon smoked paprika
- 1/2 teaspoon onion powder
- 1/2 teaspoon mustard powder

Directions:

1. Pat the eggplant dry with kitchen towels.
2. Whisk the eggs in a shallow bowl; add in the remaining ingredients. Toss the eggplant slices with the egg mixture.
3. Select the "Air Fry" function and adjust the temperature to 370 degrees F. Press the "Start" key.
4. Arrange the eggplant slices on the parchment-lined air fryer oven perforated pan.
5. Air fry the eggplant slices for 16 minutes or until crispy and cooked through, tossing them once or twice.
6. Bon appétit!

Nutrition:

- Info77 Calories,3.5g Fat,5.9g Carbs,4.7g Protei.

Montreal Chicken Drumettes

Servings: 6
Cooking Time: 25 Minutes

Ingredients:

- 2 pounds chicken drumettes
- 1 cup tomato sauce
- 2 tablespoons olive oil
- 1 teaspoon Montreal seasoning mix
- 1 tablespoon fresh basil, chopped
- 1 tablespoon fresh parsley, chopped
- 1 tablespoon fresh cilantro, chopped

Directions:

1. Select the "Air Fry" function and adjust the temperature to 375 degrees F. Press the "Start" key.
2. Place a sheet of parchment paper in the air fryer oven pan. Toss the chicken wings with the remaining ingredients.
3. Arrange the chicken wings in a single layer in the air fryer oven perforated pan.
4. Air fry the chicken wings for 10 minutes; turn them over and air fry for a further 10 minutes or until they are browned and crunchy.
5. Bon appétit!

Nutrition:

- Info257 Calories,8.7g Fat,9.4g Carbs,31.9g Protei.

Spicy Avocado Fritters

Servings: 4
Cooking Time: 10 Minutes

Ingredients:

- 2 large eggs
- 1 cup seasoned breadcrumbs
- 1/2 cup parmesan cheese, grated
- Sea salt and ground black pepper, to taste
- A few dashes of hot sauce
- 2 avocados, peeled, pitted and cut into wedges
- 2 teaspoon peanut oil (or sesame oil)

Directions:

1. In a shallow bowl, whisk the eggs until frothy. Add in the seasoned breadcrumbs, cheese, salt, black pepper, and hot sauce.
2. Dredge the avocado wedges in the breadcrumb mixture. Brush the avocado wedges with peanut oil on all sides.
3. When the display indicates "Add Food", place the avocado wedges in the air fryer oven perforated pan. Air fry them at 400 degrees F for 6 minutes.
4. Enjoy!

Nutrition:

- Info303 Calories,23.4g Fat,17.6g Carbs,9.9g Protei.

Bbq Chicken Wings

Servings: 5
Cooking Time: 25 Minutes

Ingredients:

- 1 ½ pounds chicken wings
- 1 cup BBQ sauce
- 1 tablespoon olive oil
- Kosher salt and ground black pepper, to taste

Directions:

1. Select the "Air Fry" function and adjust the temperature to 375 degrees F. Press the "Start" key.
2. Place a sheet of parchment paper in the air fryer oven pan. Toss the chicken wings with the remaining ingredients.
3. Arrange the chicken wings in a single layer in the air fryer oven perforated pan.
4. Air fry the chicken wings for 10 minutes; turn them over and air fry for a further 10 minutes or until they are browned and crunchy.
5. Bon appétit!

Nutrition:

- Info214 Calories,7.6g Fat,3.5g Carbs,30.7g Protei.

Honey Garlic Chicken Wings

Servings: 5

Cooking Time: 25 Minutes

Ingredients:

- 1 pound chicken wings
- 1/4 cup all-purpose flour
- Kosher salt and ground black pepper, to taste
- 2 teaspoons olive oil
- 1/4 cup honey
- 2 tablespoons soy sauce
- 2 garlic cloves, crushed
- 1 teaspoon red chili flakes
- 1/4 cup beer

Directions:

1. Pat the chicken wings dry. Mix the remaining ingredients until everything is well incorporated.
2. Select the "Air Fry" function and adjust the temperature to 375 degrees F. Press the "Start" key.
3. Place a sheet of parchment paper in the air fryer oven pan. Dip the chicken wings in the prepared batter.
4. Arrange the chicken wings in a single layer in the air fryer oven perforated pan.
5. Air fry the chicken wings for 10 minutes; turn them over and air fry for a further 10 minutes or until they are browned and crunchy.
6. Bon appétit!

Nutrition:

- Info258 Calories,8.4g Fat,22.3g Carbs,22.2g Protei.

Ranch Kale Chips

Servings: 2

Cooking Time: 10 Minutes

Ingredients:

- 2 cups kale leaves
- 2 teaspoons olive oil
- 1 teaspoon Ranch seasoning mix
- Kosher salt and ground black pepper, to taste

Directions:

1. Select the "Air Fry" function and adjust the temperature to 380 degrees F. Press the "Start" key.
2. Toss all the ingredients on the parchment-lined air fryer oven perforated pan.
3. Air fry the kale leaves for 6 minutes or until crispy.
4. Enjoy!

Nutrition:

- Info86 Calories,5.1g Fat,8.8g Carbs,3.4g Protei.

Favorite Sweet Potato Fries

Servings: 5

Cooking Time: 20 Minutes

Ingredients:

- 1 pound sweet potatoes, peeled and cut into sticks
- 2 tablespoons olive oil
- 1 teaspoon garlic powder
- 1 teaspoon smoked paprika
- Kosher salt and freshly cracked black pepper, to taste

Directions:

1. Toss the sweet potatoes with the remaining ingredients.
2. Select the "Air Fry" function and adjust the temperature to 400 degrees F. Press the "Start" key.
3. Arrange the sweet potatoes on the parchment-lined air fryer oven perforated pan.
4. Air fry the sweet potatoes for 15 minutes or until golden-brown and crisp.
5. Bon appétit!

Nutrition:

- Info125 Calories,5.5g Fat,17.4g Carbs,2.2g Protei.

Grape Jelly Sausage Meatballs

Servings: 5

Cooking Time: 20 Minutes

Ingredients:

- 1 pound beef sausage, crumbled
- 2 tablespoons fresh herbs, chopped
- 16 ounces grape jelly

Directions:

1. Select the "Air Fry" function and adjust the temperature to 380 degrees F. Press the "Start" key.
2. Place a sheet of parchment paper in the air fryer oven pan.
3. In a mixing bowl, thoroughly combine the sausage and herbs. Then, drop rounds of the mixture in a single layer onto the prepared pan using a small scoop.
4. Air fry the meatballs for 10 minutes. Top them with grape jelly.
5. Select the "Broil" function and cook your meatballs for a further 5 minutes or until cooked through.
6. Bon appétit!

Nutrition:

- Info453 Calories,26.4g Fat,44.1g Carbs,11.2g Protei.

Classic Cocktail Smokies

Servings: 6
Cooking Time: 15 Minutes

Ingredients:

- 1 pound cocktail wieners
- 8 ounces grape jelly
- 8 ounces tomato paste
- 1 tablespoon Dijon mustard
- 2 tablespoons fresh herbs, chopped
- 1 teaspoon whole black peppercorns, to taste

Directions:

1. Select the “Air Fry” function and adjust the temperature to 380 degrees F. Press the “Start” key.
2. Place a sheet of parchment paper in the air fryer oven pan.
3. In a mixing bowl, thoroughly combine all the ingredients. Then, place cocktail wieners in the pan.
4. Air fry the cocktail wieners for 10 minutes.
5. Bon appétit!

Nutrition:

- Info324 Calories,23.1g Fat,20.6g Carbs,9.2g Protei.

Authentic Baba Ghanoush

Servings: 8
Cooking Time: 25 Minutes

Ingredients:

- 1 ½ pounds eggplant, diced
- 4 tablespoons olive oil
- 1 medium head of garlic
- 1 tablespoon fresh lemon juice
- 1 tablespoon lemon zest
- 1/4 cup tahini
- Coarse sea salt and ground pepper, to taste
- 1 teaspoon smoked paprika

Directions:

1. Toss the eggplant with 2 tablespoons of olive oil. Place the head of garlic on a square piece of aluminum foil; bring the foil up and around the garlic.
2. Select the “Air Fry” function and adjust the temperature to 380 degrees F. Press the “Start” key.
3. Arrange the eggplant and wrapped garlic on the parchment-lined air fryer oven perforated pan.
4. Air fry the eggplant and garlic for 20 minutes or until they are tender and cooked through. Once the garlic is cool, gently squeeze on each clove (it will pop out of its skin).
5. Transfer the eggplant and garlic to the bowl of your food processor; add in the remaining ingredients and blend until creamy and smooth.
6. Bon appétit!

Nutrition:

- Info135 Calories,11g Fat,8.7g Carbs,2.5g Protei.

Favorite Cauliflower Tots

Servings: 5
Cooking Time: 15 Minutes
Ingredients:

- 1 pound cauliflower, grated
- 1 cup Mexican cheese blend, shredded
- 1/2 cup all-purpose flour
- 1 teaspoon baking powder
- 1 tablespoon butter, at room temperature
- 2 eggs, whisked
- 2 scallion stalks, chopped
- 1 cup tortilla chips, crushed
- 1/2 teaspoon cayenne pepper
- Kosher salt and ground black pepper, to taste

Directions:

1. Select the "Air Fry" function and adjust the temperature to 390 degrees F. Press the "Start" key.
2. Place a sheet of parchment paper in the air fryer oven pan. Thoroughly combine all the ingredients.
3. Form the mixture into equal balls and place them in a single layer in the air fryer oven perforated pan.
4. Air fry the cauliflower tots for 10 minutes, turning them over halfway through.
5. Bon appétit!

Nutrition:

- Info353 Calories,17.3g Fat,37.2g Carbs,13.1g Protei.

Turkey Scallion Meatballs

Servings: 6
Cooking Time: 20 Minutes
Ingredients:

- 1 pound ground turkey
- 1/2 pound ground pork
- 1/4 cup scallions, chopped
- 1/4 cup fresh parsley leaves, chopped
- 2 cloves garlic, minced
- 1 cup breadcrumbs
- 1/2 cup cream of celery soup
- 2 eggs, beaten
- 1/2 cup Pecorino Romano cheese, grated
- Sea salt and ground black pepper, to taste

Directions:

1. Select the "Air Fry" function and adjust the temperature to 380 degrees F. Press the "Start" key.
2. Place a sheet of parchment paper in the air fryer oven pan.
3. In a mixing bowl, thoroughly combine all the ingredients. Then, drop rounds of the mixture in a single layer onto the prepared pan using a small scoop.
4. Air fry the meatballs for 10 minutes.
5. Select the "Broil" function and cook your meatballs for a further 5 minutes or until cooked through.
6. Bon appétit!

Nutrition:

- Info304 Calories,18.2g Fat,7.2g Carbs,26.3g Protei.

Double Cheese Croquettes

Servings: 4
Cooking Time: 15 Minutes

Ingredients:

- 1 cup cheddar cheese, grated
- 1 cup gruyere cheese, grated
- 1 egg
- 1/2 cup all-purpose flour
- Kosher salt and ground black pepper, to taste
- 1 teaspoon olive oil

Directions:

1. Select the "Air Fry" function and adjust the temperature to 390 degrees F. Press the "Start" key.
2. Place a sheet of parchment paper in the air fryer oven pan. Thoroughly combine all the ingredients.
3. Form the mixture into equal balls and place them in a single layer in the air fryer oven perforated pan.
4. Air fry the croquettes for 10 minutes, turning them over halfway through.
5. Bon appétit!

Nutrition:

- Info337 Calories,22.7g Fat,13.6g Carbs,19g Protei.

Crispy Vidalia Rings

Servings: 4
Cooking Time: 10 Minutes

Ingredients:

- 2 large Vidalia onions, peeled and sliced
- 3/4 cup all-purpose flour
- 2 eggs
- 2 tablespoons milk
- 1 cup seasoned breadcrumbs
- 1 teaspoon smoked paprika
- Sea salt and ground black pepper, to taste
- 2 tablespoons olive oil

Directions:

1. Place the onion rings in a bowl with icy cold water; let them soak for approximately 20 minutes; drain the onion rings and pat them dry.
2. In a shallow bowl, mix flour, eggs, and milk; mix well to combine.
3. In another shallow bowl, mix bread crumbs with paprika, salt, black pepper, and olive oil. Dip the onion rings in the flour/egg mixture; then, dredge in the breadcrumb mixture. Roll to coat them evenly.
4. Spritz the air fryer pan with cooking spray; arrange the breaded onion rings on the pan.
5. Cook in the preheated air fryer oven at 390 degrees F for 8 minutes, turning them over halfway through the cooking time. Bon appétit!

Nutrition:

- Info361 Calories,12.2g Fat,46.3g Carbs,9.8g Protei.

Sausage Wonton Wraps

Servings: 6
Cooking Time: 15 Minutes
Ingredients:

- 1 pound smoked sausage, crumbled
- 2 scallion stalks, chopped
- 2 tablespoons fish sauce
- 1 teaspoon ginger-garlic paste
- 1 package wonton wrappers
- 1 egg
- 1 tablespoon olive oil

Directions:

1. In a mixing bowl, thoroughly combine crumbled sausage, scallions, fish sauce, and ginger-garlic paste.
2. Divide the mixture between wonton wrappers.
3. Whisk the egg with 1 tablespoon of olive oil and 1 tablespoon of water.
4. Fold the wonton in half. Bring up the 2 ends of the wonton and use the egg wash to stick them together. Pinch the edges and coat each wonton with egg wash.
5. Place the folded wontons on the air fryer oven perforated pan, making sure not to crowd them.
6. Select the "Air Fry" function and adjust the temperature to 380 degrees F. Press the "Start" key.
7. Air fry your wontons for 10 minutes or until they're lightly browned.
8. Bon appétit!

Nutrition:

- Info188 Calories,10.3g Fat,9g Carbs,14.6g Protei.

The Best Cheese Broccomole

Servings: 7
Cooking Time: 15 Minutes
Ingredients:

- 1 pound broccoli florets
- 2 teaspoons olive oil
- 6 ounces feta cheese, crumbled
- 1/4 cup cream of onion soup
- 1 teaspoon cayenne pepper
- 1 teaspoon garlic powder
- Kosher salt and freshly ground black pepper, to taste
- 1/2 cup Parmesan cheese, grated

Directions:

1. Toss the broccoli florets with olive oil.
2. Select the "Air Fry" function and adjust the temperature to 400 degrees F. Press the "Start" key.
3. Arrange the broccoli florets on the air fryer oven perforated pan, making sure not to crowd them.
4. Air fry the broccoli florets for 6 minutes or until cooked through, tossing them once or twice during the cooking time.
5. Blend the roasted broccoli with feta cheese, onion soup, and spices until creamy and uniform. Spoon the sauce into a lightly greased casserole dish.
6. Top the sauce with parmesan cheese and select the "Broil" function. Broil the sauce until the cheese melts.
7. Bon appétit!

Nutrition:

- Info134 Calories,8.9g Fat,7.2g Carbs,7.5g Protei.

Garlic French Bread

Servings: 4
Cooking Time: 10 Minutes
Ingredients:

- 1 loaf French bread, sliced
- 2 garlic cloves, minced
- 2 tablespoons olive oil
- Sea salt and ground black pepper, to taste
- 1 tablespoon dried parsley flakes
- 4 tablespoons Parmesan cheese, grated

Directions:

1. Select the “Toast” function and press the “Start” key.
2. Toss the bread with the remaining ingredients.
3. Toast the bread for about 3 minutes or until crispy and golden brown on the top; serve immediately.
4. Bon appétit!

Nutrition:

- Info396 Calories,10.5g Fat,61.1g Carbs,13.5g Protei.

Greek-style Pita Chips

Servings: 4
Cooking Time: 10 Minutes
Ingredients:

- 2 large pitas, cut into triangles
- 1 tablespoon extra-virgin olive oil
- 1 teaspoon Greek seasoning blend
- Coarse sea salt, to taste

Directions:

1. Select the “Air Fry” function and adjust the temperature to 330 degrees F. Press the “Start” key.
2. Place a sheet of parchment paper in the air fryer oven pan.
3. Toss the pita triangles with the remaining ingredients. Air fry the pita triangles for 6 minutes, turning them over halfway through.
4. Bon appétit!

Nutrition:

- Info103 Calories,2.3g Fat,18g Carbs,3.1g Protei.

Poultry Recipes

Restaurant-style Chicken Tenders

Servings: 4
Cooking Time: 20 Minutes

Ingredients:

- 1 tablespoon olive oil
- 1 large egg
- 1 tablespoon butter, melted
- 1 tablespoon fresh parsley leaves, chopped
- 2 garlic cloves, minced
- Sea salt and ground black pepper, to taste
- 1 ½ pounds chicken tenders
- 1 cup breadcrumbs
- 1/4 cup Pecorino cheese, grated

Directions:

1. Select the "Air Fry" function and adjust the temperature to 350 degrees F. Press the "Start" key. Lightly grease the air fryer oven perforated pan with olive oil.
2. In a shallow bowl, whisk the egg, butter, parsley, garlic, salt, and black pepper. Add the chicken tenders to the bowl and toss until well coated on all sides.
3. In another shallow bowl, mix the breadcrumbs and cheese. Roll the chicken tenders over the breadcrumb mixture until well coated on all sides.
4. When the display indicates "Add Food", place the tenders in the air fryer oven perforated pan. Air fry them for 15 minutes.
5. Bon appétit!

Nutrition:

- Info422 Calories,25.6g Fat,5.3g Carbs,39.4g Protei.

Roasted Chicken With Cauliflower

Servings: 5
Cooking Time: 20 Minutes

Ingredients:

- 1 ½ pounds boneless, skinless chicken breasts, cut into bite-sized chunks
- 1 pound cauliflower florets
- 1 tablespoon olive oil
- 1/2 teaspoon garlic powder
- 1 teaspoon paprika
- Kosher salt and ground black pepper, to taste

Directions:

1. Select the "Roast" function and adjust the temperature to 380 degrees F. Press the "Start" key.
2. Toss the chicken chunks with the other ingredients. Place the ingredients in the parchment-lined air fryer baking pan.
3. Roast the chicken and cauliflower in the preheated air fryer oven for 15 minutes or until cooked through.
4. Enjoy!

Nutrition:

- Info297 Calories,13.4g Fat,5.9g Carbs,37.2g Protei.

Creamy Turkey Salad

Servings: 5

Cooking Time: 45 Minutes + Chilling Time

Ingredients:

- 1 pound turkey breast tenderloin
- 1/2 cup mayonnaise
- 4 tablespoons Greek-style yogurt
- 1 teaspoon yellow mustard
- 1 tablespoon white vinegar
- 1 teaspoon honey
- 1 small red onion, thinly sliced
- 1 medium cucumber, diced
- 2 bell peppers, seeded and sliced
- 1 cup baby spinach

Directions:

1. Select the "Roast" function and adjust the temperature to 370 degrees F. Press the "Start" key.
2. Place the turkey in a lightly oiled baking pan. Place aluminum foil onto the drip pan.
3. Roast the turkey for about 20 minutes; flip it over and cook for 15 minutes longer or until the turkey reaches an internal temperature of 170 degrees F on a meat thermometer.
4. Let the turkey rest for 10 minutes before slicing and serving. Cut the turkey into strips and add in the other ingredients.
5. Toss to combine well and serve well-chilled. Enjoy!

Nutrition:

- Info331 Calories,23.1g Fat,6.2g Carbs,23.4g Protei.

Asian-style Glazed Duck Breast

Servings: 4

Cooking Time: 15 Minutes

Ingredients:

- 1 ½ pounds duck breasts, skin-on
- 1/4 cup honey
- 2 tablespoons soy sauce
- 2 tablespoons rice wine
- 1 teaspoon ginger, peeled and grated
- 2 tablespoons sesame oil
- Sea salt and ground black pepper, to taste
- 1 teaspoon cayenne pepper

Directions:

1. Select the "Air Fry" function and adjust the temperature to 400 degrees F. Press the "Start" key.
2. Lightly grease the air fryer oven perforated pan with olive oil. Place aluminum foil onto the drip pan.
3. Toss the duck breast with the remaining ingredients.
4. When the display indicates "Add Food", place the duck breast on the air fryer oven pan.
5. Air fry the duck breasts for about 8 minutes; flip it over and cook for 5 minutes longer or until cooked through.
6. Bon appétit!

Nutrition:

- Info378 Calories,18.3g Fat,21.2g Carbs,31.6g Protei.

Garlicky Butter Turkey

Servings: 5
Cooking Time: 40 Minutes

Ingredients:

- 1 ½ pounds turkey breast, bone-in, skin-on
- Kosher salt and freshly ground black pepper, to taste
- 4 tablespoons butter, melted
- 4 cloves garlic, minced
- 1 teaspoon dried rosemary

Directions:

1. Select the "Roast" function and adjust the temperature to 370 degrees F. Press the "Start" key.
2. Place the turkey in the air fryer oven perforated pan. Place aluminum foil onto the drip pan.
3. Roast the turkey for about 20 minutes; flip it over and cook for 15 minutes longer or until the turkey reaches an internal temperature of 170 degrees F on a meat thermometer.
4. Let the turkey rest for 10 minutes before slicing and serving. Enjoy!

Nutrition:

- Info327 Calories,16.6g Fat,1.1g Carbs,35.7g Protei.

Paprika Roast Turkey

Servings: 5
Cooking Time: 20 Minutes

Ingredients:

- 2 pounds turkey, giblet removed, rinsed, and pat dry
- 2 tablespoons olive oil
- 1 teaspoon smoked paprika
- Coarse sea salt and freshly ground black pepper, to season
- 1 teaspoon fresh rosemary, chopped
- 2 tablespoons fresh green onion, chopped
- 4 garlic cloves, chopped
- 2 bell peppers, chopped

Directions:

1. Stuff the turkey with the other ingredients. Using the rotisserie spit, push through the turkey and attach the rotisserie forks.
2. Select the "Roast" function and adjust the temperature to 350 degrees F. Set the oven to "Rotate" and set time to 3 hours. Press the "Start" key.
3. When the display indicates "Add Food", place the prepared turkey in the oven.
4. Roast the turkey until the internal temperature reaches 170 degrees F on a meat thermometer.
5. Let the turkey rest for 10 minutes before carving and serving. Enjoy!

Nutrition:

- Info425 Calories,34.4g Fat,2.1g Carbs,24.6g Protei.

Turkey Salad Sandwich

Servings: 4
Cooking Time: 45 Minutes + Chilling Time

Ingredients:

- 1 pound turkey breast tenderloin
- 1 stalk celery, chopped
- 1 cup grape tomatoes, halved
- 1 garlic clove, minced
- 2 scallions, diced
- 1/2 cup mayonnaise
- 1 teaspoon yellow mustard
- Kosher salt and ground black pepper, to taste
- 8 thin slices of bread

Directions:

1. Select the "Roast" function and adjust the temperature to 370 degrees F. Press the "Start" key.
2. Place the turkey in a lightly oiled baking pan. Place aluminum foil onto the drip pan.
3. Roast the turkey for about 20 minutes; flip it over and cook for 15 minutes longer or until the turkey reaches an internal temperature of 170 degrees F on a meat thermometer.
4. Let the turkey rest for 10 minutes before slicing. Cut the turkey into strips and add in the vegetables.
5. Now, add in the mayonnaise, mustard, salt, and black pepper; gently stir to combine well.
6. Assemble your sandwiches with well-chilled salad and enjoy!

Nutrition:

- Info536 Calories,40.2g Fat,2.8g Carbs,23.6g Protei.

Creamed Chicken Salad

Servings: 4
Cooking Time: 20 Minutes

Ingredients:

- 1 ½ pounds boneless, skinless chicken breasts, cut into bite-sized chunks
- 1 teaspoon olive oil
- Salad:
- 2 stalks celery, chopped
- 1 bell pepper, seeded and chopped
- 1/2 cup Kalamata olives, pitted and sliced
- 1 small onion, chopped
- 1 small head Romaine lettuce, torn into pieces
- Dressing:
- 6 tablespoons mayonnaise
- 2 tablespoons sour cream
- 1 teaspoon white vinegar
- 1 teaspoon Dijon mustard
- Sea salt and ground black pepper, to taste

Directions:

1. Select the "Roast" function and adjust the temperature to 380 degrees F. Press the "Start" key.
2. Toss the chicken chunks with olive oil until well coated on all sides. Place the chicken in a baking pan.
3. When the display indicates "Add Food", place the baking pan on the cooking tray.
4. Roast the chicken in the preheated air fryer oven for 15 minutes or until cooked through.
5. Toss the chicken with the remaining salad ingredients. Mix all the dressing ingredients until well combined. Dress your salad and enjoy!

Nutrition:

- Info441 Calories,27.1g Fat,10.3g Carbs,39.6g Protei.

Authentic Chicken Fajitas

Servings: 4
Cooking Time: 20 Minutes

Ingredients:

- 1 pound boneless, skinless chicken breasts, cut into strips
- 2 tablespoons olive oil
- 1 teaspoon Dijon mustard
- 2 bell peppers, seeded and sliced
- 2 garlic cloves, sliced
- 1 teaspoon ground cumin
- Sea salt and ground black pepper, to taste
- 1 teaspoon chili powder
- 1 red onion, cut into wedges
- 4 whole-wheat tortillas

Directions:

1. Select the "Roast" function and adjust the temperature to 380 degrees F. Press the "Start" key.
2. Toss the chicken strips with olive oil, mustard, bell peppers, garlic, cumin, salt, black pepper, and chili powder.
3. Place the chicken and peppers in a baking pan. Place aluminum foil onto the drip pan.
4. When the display indicates "Add Food", place the baking pan on the cooking tray.
5. Roast the chicken and peppers in the preheated air fryer oven for 15 minutes or until the chicken reaches an internal temperature of 165 degrees F on a meat thermometer.
6. Assemble your fajitas with onion wedges and tortillas. Enjoy!

Nutrition:

- Info413 Calories,21.6g Fat,25.7g Carbs,28.8g Protei.

Curried Chicken Cups

Servings: 4
Cooking Time: 20 Minutes

Ingredients:

- 1 pound chicken breast, boneless, skinless, and chopped
- 1 tablespoon butter, melted
- 2 tablespoons scallions, chopped
- 1 teaspoon curry paste
- 2 cups self-rising flour
- 2 large eggs, beaten
- Sea salt and ground black pepper, to taste

Directions:

1. Select the "Bake" function and adjust the temperature to 380 degrees F and the time to 15 minutes. Press the "Start" key.
2. Meanwhile, brush silicone muffin cups with nonstick cooking oil. Mix all the ingredients until well combined. Divide the mixture between the muffin cups.
3. When the display indicates "Add Food", place the muffin cups on the cooking tray.
4. Bake the muffins in the preheated air fryer oven until cooked through. Bon appétit!

Nutrition:

- Info485 Calories,16.4g Fat,48.1g Carbs,33.3g Protei.

Kid-friendly Chicken Nuggets

Servings: 5
Cooking Time: 20 Minutes

Ingredients:

- 1 teaspoon olive oil
- 2 pounds boneless, skinless chicken breasts, cut into 1-inch-thick strips
- 1 egg, beaten
- 1 cup all-purpose flour
- Coarse sea salt and ground black pepper, to taste
- 1 cup tortilla chips, crushed

Directions:

1. Select the “Air Fry” function and adjust the temperature to 350 degrees F. Press the “Start” key. Then, grease the air fryer oven perforated pan with olive oil.
2. Pat the chicken dry and set it aside.
3. In a shallow bowl, whisk the egg until pale and frothy; gradually add in the flour, salt, and black pepper. Add the chicken tenders to the bowl and toss until well coated on all sides.
4. In another shallow bowl, place the crushed tortilla chips. Roll the chicken strips over the crushed tortilla chips until well coated on all sides.
5. When the display indicates “Add Food”, place the tenders in the air fryer oven perforated pan. Air fry them for 15 minutes.
6. Serve warm and enjoy!

Nutrition:

- Info440 Calories,13.2g Fat,37.5g Carbs,42.4g Protei.

Classic Chicken Cutlets

Servings: 4
Cooking Time: 25 Minutes

Ingredients:

- 1 ½ pounds chicken breasts, sliced
- 1 tablespoon butter, melted
- 2 eggs, whisked
- 1/2 teaspoon cayenne pepper
- Kosher salt and ground black pepper, to taste
- 1 cup seasoned breadcrumbs

Directions:

1. Select the “Air Fry” function and adjust the temperature to 360 degrees F. Press the “Start” key.
2. Toss the chicken with the remaining ingredients.
3. When the display indicates “Add Food”, place the chicken tenders in the parchment-lined air fryer oven pan.
4. Air Fry the chicken for about 10 minutes; flip it over and cook for 10 minutes longer or until the chicken reaches an internal temperature of 160 degrees F on a meat thermometer.
5. Bon appétit!

Nutrition:

- Info465 Calories,20.7g Fat,21.1g Carbs,40.7g Protei.

Favorite Turkey Meatballs

Servings: 4
Cooking Time: 20 Minutes

Ingredients:

- 1 tablespoon olive oil
- 1 pound ground turkey
- 1/2 cup Pecorino cheese, grated
- 1/4 cup breadcrumbs
- 2 tablespoons parsley, chopped
- 2 tablespoons basil, chopped
- 2 tablespoons chives, chopped
- Kosher salt and ground black pepper, to taste
- 1 teaspoon garlic, minced
- 1 teaspoon cayenne pepper
- 1 medium egg

Directions:

1. Select the "Air Fry" function and adjust the temperature to 350 degrees F. Press the "Start" key.
2. Place a sheet of parchment paper in the air fryer oven pan.
3. In a mixing bowl, thoroughly combine the remaining ingredients. Then, drop rounds of the mixture in a single layer onto the prepared pan using a small scoop.
4. Air fry the meatballs for 10 minutes; turn the meatballs over and increase the temperature to 400 degrees F. Air fry for a further 5 minutes to brown the outsides of the meatballs, until they reach an internal temperature of 165 degrees F.
5. Bon appétit!

Nutrition:

- Info291 Calories,18.6g Fat,3.3g Carbs,28.4g Protei.

Classic Turkey Burgers

Servings: 4
Cooking Time: 20 Minutes

Ingredients:

- 1 tablespoon olive oil
- 1 pound ground chicken
- 1/2 cup crackers, crushed
- 1 small onion, chopped
- 2 cloves garlic, minced
- 1 egg, beaten
- Sea salt and ground black pepper, to taste

Directions:

1. Select the "Air Fry" function and adjust the temperature to 340 degrees F. Press the "Start" key.
2. Place a sheet of parchment paper in the air fryer oven pan.
3. Mix all the ingredients until well combined. Shape the mixture into four patties and place them in a single layer in the air fryer oven perforated pan.
4. Air fry the turkey burgers for 15 minutes or until they reach an internal temperature of 165 degrees F.
5. Bon appétit!

Nutrition:

- Info322 Calories,23.2g Fat,3.6g Carbs,23.8g Protei.

Mediterranean Chicken Salad

Servings: 4
Cooking Time: 45 Minutes
Ingredients:

- 1 ½ pounds skinless, boneless chicken breasts
- 3 tablespoons olive oil
- 2 tablespoons freshly squeezed lemon juice
- 1 tablespoon white vinegar
- 1 teaspoon yellow mustard
- 2 tablespoons fresh cilantro, chopped
- 2 tablespoons fresh basil, chopped
- 1 teaspoon dried oregano
- 2 garlic cloves, pressed
- 1 bell pepper, seeded and diced
- Sea salt and ground black pepper, to taste
- 2 cups Romaine lettuce leaves, torn into leaves
- 1 cucumber, diced
- 1 cup cherry tomatoes, halved
- 1 red onion, thinly sliced
- 3 ounces Kalamata olives pitted and sliced

Directions:

1. Select the “Roast” function and adjust the temperature to 360 degrees F. Press the “Start” key.
2. When the display indicates “Add Food”, place the chicken in the parchment-lined air fryer oven pan.
3. Roast the chicken for about 20 minutes; flip it over and cook for 20 minutes longer or until the chicken reaches an internal temperature of 160 degrees F on a meat thermometer.
4. Transfer the chicken breast to a cutting board and let it rest for 10 minutes before slicing into strips.
5. Toss the chicken strips with the remaining ingredients and place your salad in the refrigerator until ready to serve. Bon appétit!

Nutrition:

- Info475 Calories,32g Fat,11.8g Carbs,36.6g Protei.

Rotisserie-style Chicken

Servings: 7
Cooking Time: 50 Minutes
Ingredients:

- 3 pounds whole chicken, tied
- 2 tablespoons olive oil
- 1 teaspoon smoked paprika
- 1 teaspoon garlic powder
- 1 teaspoon onion powder
- 1 teaspoon dried thyme
- Kosher salt and freshly ground black pepper, to taste

Directions:

1. Using the rotisserie spit, push through the chicken and attach the rotisserie forks.
2. Select the “Roast” function and adjust the temperature to 365 degrees F. Set the oven to “Rotate” and set the time to 1 hour. Press the “Start” key.
3. When the display indicates “Add Food”, place the prepared chicken in the oven.
4. Roast the chicken until it reaches 165 degrees F in the breast and 185 degrees F in the thighs.
5. Let the chicken rest for 10 minutes before carving and serving. Bon appétit!

Nutrition:

- Info456 Calories,33.1g Fat,0.8g Carbs,36.3g Protei.

Herb Chicken Cutlets

Servings: 4
Cooking Time: 25 Minutes
Ingredients:

- 1 ½ pounds boneless, skinless chicken fillets
- 1 tablespoon Dijon mustard
- 4 tablespoons mayonnaise
- 1/2 cup crackers, crushed
- Kosher salt and ground black pepper, to taste
- 1 teaspoon dried rosemary
- 1 teaspoon dried thyme
- 1/2 teaspoon garlic powder
- 1 teaspoon hot paprika

Directions:

1. Select the "Air Fry" function and adjust the temperature to 360 degrees F. Press the "Start" key.
2. Toss the chicken with the remaining ingredients in the air fryer oven perforated pan. Place aluminum foil onto the drip pan.
3. Air fry the chicken for about 10 minutes; flip it over and cook for 10 minutes longer or until the chicken reaches an internal temperature of 160 degrees F on a meat thermometer.
4. Bon appétit!

Nutrition:

- Info472 Calories,36.2g Fat,2.5g Carbs,32.3g Protei.

Classic Chicken Fingers

Servings: 4
Cooking Time: 20 Minutes
Ingredients:

- 1 tablespoon olive oil
- 1 ½ pounds skinless, boneless chicken breast, cut into 1/2-inch strips
- 1 egg, beaten
- 1 cup buttermilk
- 1 cup all-purpose flour
- 1 teaspoon onion powder
- 1 teaspoon garlic powder
- 1 teaspoon red pepper flakes
- Sea salt and ground black pepper, to taste
- 1 cup Ritz crackers, crushed

Directions:

1. Select the "Air Fry" function and adjust the temperature to 350 degrees F. Press the "Start" key. Now, grease the air fryer oven perforated pan with olive oil.
2. Pat the chicken dry and set it aside.
3. In a shallow bowl, whisk the egg and buttermilk; gradually add in the flour and spices. Add the chicken tenders to the bowl and toss until well coated on all sides.
4. In another shallow bowl, place the crushed crackers. Roll the chicken strips over the crushed crackers until well coated on all sides.
5. When the display indicates "Add Food", place the tenders in the air fryer oven perforated pan. Air fry them for 15 minutes.
6. Serve warm and enjoy!

Nutrition:

- Info401 Calories,9.9g Fat,29.5g Carbs,45.3g Protei.

Easy Chicken Burgers

Servings: 4

Cooking Time: 20 Minutes

Ingredients:

- 1 pound ground chicken
- 1 tablespoon olive oil
- 1 egg, whisked
- 1 cup bread crumbs
- 1/2 cup parmesan cheese, grated
- 1 small onion, finely chopped
- 2 garlic cloves, minced
- 1 teaspoon cayenne pepper
- Kosher salt and ground black pepper, to taste

Directions:

1. Select the "Air Fry" function and adjust the temperature to 340 degrees F. Press the "Start" key.
2. Place a sheet of parchment paper in the air fryer oven pan.
3. Mix all the ingredients until well combined. Shape the mixture into four patties and place them in a single layer in the air fryer oven perforated pan.
4. Air fry the chicken burgers for 15 minutes or until they reach an internal temperature of 165 degrees F.
5. Bon appétit!

Nutrition:

- Info305 Calories,26.7g Fat,17.5g Carbs,10.7g Protei.

Butter Rosemary Chicken Cutlets

Servings: 4

Cooking Time: 25 Minutes

Ingredients:

- 2 tablespoons butter, at room temperature
- 1 ½ pounds boneless, skinless chicken breasts, cut into cutlets
- 1 tablespoon mustard
- 1 tablespoon soy sauce
- 1 teaspoon garlic, minced
- Kosher salt and ground black pepper, to taste
- 1 teaspoon Italian seasoning mix

Directions:

1. Select the "Air Fry" function and adjust the temperature to 360 degrees F. Press the "Start" key.
2. Toss the chicken cutlets with the remaining ingredients and place them in the air fryer oven perforated pan. Place aluminum foil onto the drip pan.
3. Air fry the chicken for about 10 minutes; flip it over and cook for 10 minutes longer or until the chicken reaches an internal temperature of 160 degrees F on a meat thermometer.
4. Bon appétit!

Nutrition:

- Info437 Calories,32.2g Fat,2.9g Carbs,32.4g Protei.

Fish And Seafood Recipes

Ultimate Tuna Melts

Servings: 4
Cooking Time: 15 Minutes
Ingredients:

- 12 ounces canned albacore tuna, drained
- 4 Hawaiian sweet rolls, split
- 1/2 cup mayonnaise
- 4 slices cheddar cheese
- 2 tablespoons scallions, chopped

Directions:

1. Select the “Broil” function and adjust the temperature to 400 degrees F. Set the time to 12 minutes. Press the “Start” key.
2. Assemble the sandwiches by laying out the rolls and, then, adding the remaining ingredients. Spritz the sandwiches with nonstick oil.
3. When the display indicates “Add Food”, place the sandwiches in the parchment-lined air fryer oven perforated pan.
4. Bake your sandwiches for 6 minutes, flip them over, spritz with nonstick oil and continue baking for 6 minutes more.
5. Serve immediately.

Nutrition:

- Info445 Calories,32.2g Fat,15.1g Carbs,2.6g Protei.

Sea Scallop Salad

Servings: 4
Cooking Time: 15 Minutes
Ingredients:

- 1 pound sea scallops
- Kosher salt and ground black pepper, to taste
- 1 teaspoon cayenne pepper
- 1/4 cup extra-virgin olive oil
- 2 tablespoons fresh chives, chopped
- 2 tablespoons fresh mint, chopped
- 2 tablespoons fresh parsley, chopped
- 2 tablespoons balsamic vinegar
- 1 red onion, chopped
- 2 garlic cloves, minced
- 2 teaspoons honey
- 1 teaspoon Dijon mustard
- 2 cups mix salad greens
- 1 carrot, julienned
- 1 bell pepper, sliced
- 1 cup grape tomatoes, halved

Directions:

1. Select the “Air Fry” function and adjust the temperature to 400 degrees F. Press the “Start” key.
2. When the display indicates “Add Food”, place the sea scallops in the air fryer oven perforated pan.
3. Air fry the sea scallops for 10 minutes or until pink and opaque. Add in the remaining ingredients and toss to combine. Bon appétit!

Nutrition:

- Info259 Calories,14g Fat,17.3g Carbs,15.5g Protei.

Cajun Crab Sticks

Servings: 4
Cooking Time: 15 Minutes

Ingredients:

- 1 pound crab sticks
- 1 teaspoon garlic, minced
- 1 tablespoon lemon juice
- 1 teaspoon Dijon mustard
- 1 tablespoon butter, melted
- 1 teaspoon Cajun seasoning mix
- Sea salt and ground black pepper, to taste

Directions:

1. Select the "Air Fry" function and adjust the temperature to 380 degrees F. Press the "Start" key.
2. In a mixing bowl, toss the crab sticks with the remaining ingredients.
3. When the display indicates "Add Food", place the crab sticks in the air fryer oven perforated pan.
4. Air fry the crab sticks for 12 minutes or until pink and opaque.
5. Bon appétit!

Nutrition:

- Info138 Calories,4.1g Fat,0.8g Carbs,20.5g Protei.

Mediterranean-style Shrimp Salad

Servings: 4
Cooking Time: 15 Minutes + Chilling Time

Ingredients:

- 1 pound shrimp, peeled and deveined
- 1/4 cup extra-virgin olive oil
- 1 teaspoon Dijon mustard
- 2 teaspoons lime juice
- Sea salt and freshly ground black pepper, to taste
- 1 small red onion, chopped
- 2 tablespoons fresh dill, chopped
- 2 tablespoons fresh parsley, chopped
- 2 cups Romaine lettuce

Directions:

1. Select the "Air Fry" function and adjust the temperature to 400 degrees F. Press the "Start" key.
2. In a mixing bowl, toss the shrimp with 1 teaspoon of olive oil.
3. When the display indicates "Add Food", place the shrimp in the air fryer oven perforated pan.
4. Air fry the shrimp for 7 to 8 minutes or until pink and opaque. Toss your shrimp with the other salad ingredients and serve well-chilled.
5. Bon appétit!

Nutrition:

- Info243 Calories,14.8g Fat,4.6g Carbs,23.9g Protei.

Cajun Squid Rings

Servings: 4
Cooking Time: 15 Minutes
Ingredients:

- 1 pound squid rings
- 1 teaspoon onion powder
- 1 teaspoon garlic powder
- 1/2 cup spelt flour
- 1/2 cup buttermilk
- 1 teaspoon Cajun seasoning mix
- Sea salt and ground black pepper, to season
- 2 teaspoons olive oil

Directions:

1. In a mixing bowl, thoroughly combine all the ingredients, except for the squid rings.
2. Dredge the squid rings in the buttermilk mixture.
3. Select the "Air Fry" function and adjust the temperature to 390 degrees F. Press the "Start" key.
4. Arrange the squid rings on the air fryer oven perforated pan, making sure not to crowd them. Air fry the squid rings for 10 minutes or until golden brown.
5. Bon appétit!

Nutrition:

- Info215 Calories,4.1g Fat,21.6g Carbs,19.2g Protei.

Crab And Pea Patties

Servings: 4
Cooking Time: 15 Minutes
Ingredients:

- 3/4 pound lump crab meat
- 1 cup canned green peas, drained
- 1/2 cup seasoned breadcrumbs
- 1/4 cup celery, diced
- 4 tablespoons green onions, chopped
- 4 tablespoons mayonnaise
- 1 teaspoon brown mustard
- 2 tablespoons ketchup
- 4 tablespoons cheddar cheese, shredded
- 1 teaspoon smoked paprika
- 1 teaspoon dried oregano
- Kosher salt and ground black pepper, to taste

Directions:

1. Select the "Air Fry" function and adjust the temperature to 370 degrees F. Press the "Start" key.
2. Place a sheet of parchment paper in the air fryer oven pan.
3. Thoroughly combine all the ingredients in a mixing bowl. Form the mixture into patties and place them in a single layer in the air fryer oven perforated pan.
4. Air fry the patties for 10 minutes. Serve immediately and enjoy!

Nutrition:

- Info375 Calories,22.2g Fat,18.8g Carbs,21.2g Protei.

Favorite Halibut Steaks

Servings: 4
Cooking Time: 10 Minutes

Ingredients:

- 1 ½ pounds halibut steaks
- 2 tablespoons butter, melted
- 2 tablespoons lemon juice
- 1 tablespoon fresh basil, minced
- 1 tablespoon fresh mint, minced
- 1 tablespoon fresh parsley, minced
- 1/2 teaspoon garlic salt
- 1 teaspoon cayenne pepper
- 1/2 teaspoon ground black pepper

Directions:

1. Select the "Air Fry" function and adjust the temperature to 400 degrees F. Set the oven to "Rotate" and set time to 10 minutes. Press the "Start" key.
2. In a mixing bowl, toss the fish with the other ingredients.
3. When the display indicates "Add Food", place the fish in the rotisserie basket. Roast the fish until it flakes easily with a fork.
4. Bon appétit!

Nutrition:

- Info253 Calories,14.4g Fat,7.9g Carbs,25.5g Protei.

Street-style Fish Fritters

Servings: 5
Cooking Time: 15 Minutes

Ingredients:

- 1 ½ pounds haddock, chopped (or any other mild white fish)
- 2 ounces bacon bits
- 1 zucchini, grated
- 1 medium onion, diced
- 2 garlic cloves, minced
- 1 chili pepper, chopped
- 2 medium eggs, beaten
- ¼ cup full-fat milk
- 1 cup instant oats
- 1 teaspoon baking powder

Directions:

1. Select the "Air Fry" function and adjust the temperature to 390 degrees F. Press the "Start" key.
2. Place a sheet of parchment paper in the air fryer oven pan. Thoroughly combine all the ingredients.
3. Form the mixture into four patties and place them in a single layer in the air fryer oven perforated pan.
4. Air fry the patties for 12 minutes, turning them over halfway through. Serve warm and enjoy!

Nutrition:

- Info315 Calories,9.4g Fat,24.8g Carbs,32.2g Protei.

Creole Catfish Fillets

Servings: 4
Cooking Time: 15 Minutes
Ingredients:

- 1 pound catfish fillets
- 2 eggs, beaten
- 1/2 cup all-purpose flour
- 1/2 cup breadcrumbs
- 1 teaspoon Creole seasoning mix
- 2 teaspoons olive oil
- 1 tablespoon fresh parsley, chopped
- 1 tablespoon fresh cilantro, chopped

Directions:

1. Select the "Air Fry" function and adjust the temperature to 400 degrees F. Set the time to 10 minutes. Press the "Start" key.
2. Pat the fish dry. In a shallow bowl, whisk the eggs with the flour. In a shallow bowl, mix the remaining ingredients.
3. Dip the fish into the egg mixture. Then, roll the fish over the breadcrumb mixture.
4. When the display indicates "Add Food", place the fish in the parchment-lined air fryer oven perforated pan.
5. Air fry the fish until it flakes easily with a fork. Bon appétit!

Nutrition:

- Info244 Calories,7.8g Fat,15.4g Carbs,23.5g Protei.

Paprika Tuna Steaks

Servings: 4
Cooking Time: 15 Minutes
Ingredients:

- 1 ½ pounds tuna steaks
- Sea salt and ground black pepper, to season
- 1 teaspoon smoked paprika
- 2 tablespoons butter
- 1 teaspoon ginger, peeled and minced
- 2 cloves garlic, minced
- 2 tablespoons honey
- 2 tablespoons soy sauce

Directions:

1. Select the "Air Fry" function and adjust the temperature to 400 degrees F. Set the oven to "Rotate" and set time to 10 minutes. Press the "Start" key.
2. In a mixing bowl, toss the tuna steaks with the other ingredients.
3. When the display indicates "Add Food", place the fish in the rotisserie basket. Roast the tuna steaks until they flake easily with a fork.
4. Bon appétit!

Nutrition:

- Info295 Calories,9.1g Fat,12.7g Carbs,38.4g Protei.

Favorite Seafood Fritters

Servings: 4
Cooking Time: 15 Minutes

Ingredients:

- 1 pound shrimp, peeled and deveined
- 1 large sweet onion, chopped
- 1 teaspoon garlic, pressed
- 1 bell pepper, chopped
- 1/2 cup all-purpose flour
- 1/2 cup tortilla chips, crushed
- 2 teaspoons butter, melted
- 1 teaspoon baking powder
- 1 teaspoon Cajun seasoning mix
- Sea salt and freshly ground black pepper, to taste
- 1 teaspoon paprika
- 1 teaspoon stone-ground mustard
- 2 large eggs, beaten
- 1/4 cup cream of celery soup

Directions:

1. Select the "Air Fry" function and adjust the temperature to 370 degrees F. Press the "Start" key.
2. Place a sheet of parchment paper in the air fryer oven pan.
3. Thoroughly combine all the ingredients in a mixing bowl. Form the mixture into equal patties and place them in a single layer in the air fryer oven perforated pan.
4. Air fry the fritters for 13 minutes. Serve warm and enjoy!

Nutrition:

- Info345 Calories,10.4g Fat,32.8g Carbs,30.1g Protei.

Restaurant-style Calamari

Servings: 4
Cooking Time: 10 Minutes

Ingredients:

- 1/4 cup cream of onion soup
- 2 medium eggs, beaten
- 1/2 cup all-purpose flour
- 1/2 cup tortilla chips, crushed
- Sea salt and ground black pepper, to taste
- 1 teaspoon red pepper flakes, crushed
- 1 teaspoon garlic powder
- 2 teaspoon olive oil
- 1 pound squid rings

Directions:

1. In a shallow bowl, mix the soup, egg, and flour. In another shallow bowl, place tortilla chips, spices, and olive oil.
2. Dredge the squid rings in the egg mixture. Then, dip the squid rings in crushed tortilla chips, coating them completely.
3. Select the "Air Fry" function and adjust the temperature to 390 degrees F. Press the "Start" key.
4. Arrange the squid rings on the air fryer oven perforated pan, making sure not to crowd them. Air fry the squid rings for 10 minutes or until golden brown.
5. Bon appétit!

Nutrition:

- Info295 Calories,9.5g Fat,27.3g Carbs,23.5g Protei.

Classic Fried Sea Scallops

Servings: 4
Cooking Time: 15 Minutes
Ingredients:

- 1 pound sea scallops
- 1 teaspoon garlic, minced
- 1 teaspoon onion powder
- 2 teaspoons olive oil
- Kosher salt and ground black pepper, to taste
- 1 teaspoon paprika
- 1 teaspoon dried basil
- 1 teaspoon dried oregano

Directions:

1. Select the “Air Fry” function and adjust the temperature to 400 degrees F. Press the “Start” key.
2. In a mixing bowl, toss the sea scallops with the other ingredients.
3. When the display indicates “Add Food”, place the sea scallops in the air fryer oven perforated pan.
4. Air fry the sea scallops for 10 minutes or until pink and opaque.
5. Bon appétit!

Nutrition:

- Info346 Calories,6.8g Fat,4.6g Carbs,37.1g Protei.

Mini Smoked Salmon Frittatas

Servings: 4
Cooking Time: 15 Minutes
Ingredients:

- 12 ounces smoked salmon, chopped
- 6 eggs
- 1 ounce butter, softened
- 2 ounces cream cheese
- 1/4 cup sour cream
- 2 tablespoons fresh parsley, chopped
- 2 tablespoons fresh basil, chopped
- 2 tablespoons fresh scallions, chopped
- Sea salt and freshly ground black pepper, to season

Directions:

1. Select the “Bake” function and adjust the temperature to 350 degrees F and the time to 13 minutes. Press the “Start” key.
2. Meanwhile, brush silicone muffin cups with nonstick oil. Mix all the ingredients until well combined. Divide the mixture between the muffin cups.
3. When the display indicates “Add Food”, place the muffin cups on the cooking tray in the center position.
4. Cook the mini fritters to your desired texture and serve warm. Bon appétit!

Nutrition:

- Info355 Calories,24.5g Fat,2.5g Carbs,27.3g Protei.

Father's Day Fish Tacos

Servings: 4
Cooking Time: 15 Minutes
Ingredients:

- 1 pound tilapia fillets (or other mild white fish)
- 1 tablespoon butter, melted
- 1 teaspoon red pepper flakes
- 1/2 teaspoon cumin
- 1 teaspoon paprika
- Sea salt and ground black pepper, to taste
- 1 teaspoon Mexican oregano
- 1 teaspoon garlic, minced
- Tacos:
- 4 medium flour tortillas
- 1 avocado, pitted and sliced
- 1 tomato, thinly sliced
- 1 red onion, thinly sliced

Directions:

1. Select the "Air Fry" function and adjust the temperature to 400 degrees F. Set the oven to "Rotate" and set time to 10 minutes. Press the "Start" key.
2. In a mixing bowl, toss the fish with the melted butter, spices, and garlic.
3. When the display indicates "Add Food", place the fish in the rotisserie basket.
4. Roast the fish until it is thoroughly cooked. Cut your fish into strips; assemble your tacos with the fish and other ingredients.
5. Bon appétit!

Nutrition:

- Info363 Calories,15.1g Fat,29.6g Carbs,28.5g Protei.

Favorite Seafood Sliders

Servings: 4
Cooking Time: 20 Minutes
Ingredients:

- 12 ounces shrimp, chopped
- 2 large eggs, whisked
- Zest of 1 lemon
- 1/2 cup seasoned breadcrumbs
- 1/2 cup parmesan cheese, preferably freshly grated
- 1 large onion, chopped
- 2 garlic cloves, minced
- 1/2 teaspoon dried oregano
- 1/2 teaspoon dried dill
- Kosher salt and freshly cracked black pepper, to taste
- 2 tablespoons olive oil
- 8 dinner rolls

Directions:

1. Select the "Air Fry" function and adjust the temperature to 390 degrees F. Press the "Start" key.
2. Place a sheet of parchment paper in the air fryer oven pan. Thoroughly combine all the ingredients, except for the dinner rolls.
3. Form the mixture into eight patties and place them in a single layer in the air fryer oven perforated pan.
4. Air fry the patties for 15 minutes, turning them over halfway through. Assemble your slider with warm patties and dinner rolls and serve immediately.
5. Bon appétit!

Nutrition:

- Info415 Calories,16.9g Fat,36.5g Carbs,29.7g Protei.

Greek-style Pita Wraps

Servings: 4
Cooking Time: 15 Minutes
Ingredients:

- 1 pound haddock fillets
- 2 ounces anchovy fillets
- 2 teaspoons olive oil
- 1/4 cup mayonnaise
- 2 ounces feta cheese, crumbled
- Sea salt and ground black pepper, to taste
- 2 cups mixed greens
- 1 red onion, thinly sliced
- 4 pita breads

Directions:

1. Select the "Air Fry" function and adjust the temperature to 400 degrees F. Set the oven to "Rotate" and set time to 10 minutes. Press the "Start" key.
2. Toss the fish with olive oil and place it in the rotisserie basket. Air fry the fish for 10 minutes or until it is thoroughly cooked.
3. Cut the fish into strips.
4. Assemble the pita wraps with warm fish strips and the remaining ingredients. Serve immediately and enjoy!

Nutrition:

- Info315 Calories,12.3g Fat,18.7g Carbs,28.7g Protei.

Roasted Salmon With Cauliflower

Servings: 4
Cooking Time: 15 Minutes
Ingredients:

- 1 pound salmon steaks
- 1 pound cauliflower florets
- 1 teaspoon garlic powder
- 1 teaspoon onion powder
- 1/2 teaspoon turmeric powder
- 2 tablespoons olive oil
- Sea salt and ground black pepper, to taste
- Juice of 1 lemon

Directions:

1. Select the "Air Fry" function and adjust the temperature to 400 degrees F. Press the "Start" key.
2. When the display indicates "Add Food", toss all the ingredients into the air fryer oven perforated pan.
3. Roast the salmon and cauliflower for 10 minutes or until cooked through. Serve warm and enjoy!

Nutrition:

- Info285 Calories,13.9g Fat,8.8g Carbs,32.5g Protei.

Greek-style Fish Sticks

Servings: 4
Cooking Time: 15 Minutes

Ingredients:

- 1 pound codfish fillets, cut into strips
- 2 teaspoons olive oil
- 1 large egg
- 4 tablespoons Greek-style yogurt
- 1 teaspoon hot paprika
- 1 teaspoon Greek oregano
- Kosher salt and ground black pepper, to taste
- 1/2 cup all-purpose flour
- 1 cup seasoned breadcrumbs
- 1/4 cup parmesan cheese, grated

Directions:

1. In a shallow bowl, mix the olive oil, egg, yogurt, spices. In another shallow bowl, mix the breadcrumbs and parmesan cheese, and flour.
2. Dredge the fish strips in the egg/yogurt mixture. Then, dip the strips in the breadcrumb mixture, coating them completely and shaking off any excess.
3. Select the "Air Fry" function and adjust the temperature to 400 degrees F. Press the "Start" key.
4. Arrange the fish strips on the air fryer oven perforated pan, making sure not to crowd them. Air fry the fish for 10 minutes.
5. Bon appétit!

Nutrition:

- Info325 Calories,6.4g Fat,34.8g Carbs,24.7g Protei.

Spicy Peppery Tiger Prawn Salad

Servings: 4
Cooking Time: 10 Minutes

Ingredients:

- 1 pound tiger prawns, peeled and deveined
- 2 garlic cloves, minced
- 2 tablespoons fresh parsley, roughly chopped
- 2 tablespoons fresh cilantro, roughly chopped
- 2 scallion stalks, chopped
- 2 bell peppers, sliced
- 1 red chili pepper, sliced
- Sea salt and ground black pepper, to taste
- 1/4 cup extra-virgin olive oil
- 1 teaspoon yellow mustard

Directions:

1. Select the "Air Fry" function and adjust the temperature to 390 degrees F. Press the "Start" key.
2. In a mixing bowl, toss the shrimp with 1 teaspoon of olive oil.
3. When the display indicates "Add Food", place your prawns in the air fryer oven perforated pan.
4. Air fry your prawns for 7 to 8 minutes or until pink and opaque. Toss your prawns with the other salad ingredients and serve well-chilled.
5. Bon appétit!

Nutrition:

- Info253 Calories,14.4g Fat,7.9g Carbs,25.5g Protei.

Pork And Beef Recipes

Hot And Juicy Beef Brisket

Servings: 4
Cooking Time: 50 Minutes
Ingredients:

- 1 ½ pounds beef brisket
- 2 tablespoons brown sugar
- Kosher salt and ground black pepper, to taste
- 1 teaspoon chili powder
- 1 teaspoon garlic powder
- 1 teaspoon hot paprika
- 2 tablespoons butter, melted
- 2 tablespoons scallions, sliced thinly
- 2 garlic cloves, smashed
- 1/2 cup ketchup
- 2 tablespoons white vinegar
- 1 tablespoon stone-ground mustard
- 2 tablespoons molasses

Directions:

1. Select the "Air Fry" function and adjust the temperature to 350 degrees F. Press the "Start" key.
2. Toss the beef brisket with the other ingredients. Place aluminum foil onto the drip pan.
3. When the display indicates "Add Food", place the beef in the air fryer oven perforated pan. Cook the beef brisket for about 25 minutes.
4. Turn the temperature to 390 degrees F. Turn it over and continue to cook for 25 minutes more.
5. Serve warm and enjoy!

Nutrition:

- Info484 Calories,31.9g Fat,23.2g Carbs,26.2g Protei.

Country-style Ribs

Servings: 5
Cooking Time: 40 Minutes + Marinating Time
Ingredients:

- 2 pounds country-style pork ribs
- 2 garlic cloves, minced
- 2 chili peppers, minced
- Sea salt and ground black pepper, to taste
- 1 teaspoon cumin
- 1 tablespoon brown sugar
- 1/2 cup tomato sauce
- 2 tablespoons olive oil
- 1 tablespoon Worcestershire sauce

Directions:

1. Place all the ingredients in a ceramic dish. Let it marinate for at least 1 hour.
2. Select the "Air Fry" function and adjust the temperature to 350 degrees F. Press the "Start" key. Place aluminum foil onto the drip pan.
3. When the display indicates "Add Food", add the pork ribs to the rotisserie basket. Cook the pork ribs for about 35 minutes or until they are thoroughly cooked.
4. Bon appétit!

Nutrition:

- Info443 Calories,27.1g Fat,10.1g Carbs,36.4g Protei.

Jamaican-style Pork

Servings: 4
Cooking Time: 25 Minutes + Marinating Time

Ingredients:

- 1 pound pork butt, sliced
- 2 tablespoons olive oil
- 2 Scotch bonnet peppers, chopped
- 1/4 cup apple cider vinegar
- 2 tablespoons soy sauce
- 2 tablespoons brown sugar
- 1 teaspoon allspice
- 1 teaspoon cinnamon

Directions:

1. Add all the ingredients to a ceramic or glass bowl. Allow the pork to marinate for at least 3 hours.
2. Select the "Air Fry" function and adjust the temperature to 390 degrees F. Press the "Start" key. Place aluminum foil onto the drip pan.
3. When the display indicates "Add Food", place the pork in the air fryer oven perforated pan. Reserve the marinade. Cook the pork for about 10 minutes.
4. Baste the pork with the reserved marinade and continue to roast for about 10 minutes or until cooked through. Serve immediately and enjoy!

Nutrition:

- Info386 Calories,28.6g Fat,9.1g Carbs,20.5g Protei.

Chinese-style Pork Meatballs

Servings: 4
Cooking Time: 20 Minutes

Ingredients:

- 1 pound ground pork
- 1 egg
- 1/2 cup crushed crackers
- 1 small onion, chopped
- 2 cloves garlic, minced
- 2 tablespoons cilantro, chopped
- 2 tablespoons parsley, chopped
- Sea salt and freshly ground black pepper, to taste
- Five-spice powder (optional)
- 2 tablespoons soy sauce
- 2 tablespoons tomato sauce
- A dash of Tabasco sauce

Directions:

1. Select the "Air Fry" function and adjust the temperature to 380 degrees F. Press the "Start" key.
2. Place a sheet of parchment paper in the air fryer oven pan.
3. In a mixing bowl, thoroughly combine all the ingredients. Then, drop rounds of the mixture in a single layer onto the prepared pan using a small scoop.
4. Air fry the meatballs for 10 minutes.
5. Select the "Broil" function and cook your meatballs for a further 5 minutes or until cooked through.
6. Bon appétit!

Nutrition:

- Info397 Calories,28.2g Fat,12.5g Carbs,22.8g Protei.

Old-fashioned Mini Meatloaves

Servings: 4
Cooking Time: 30 Minutes

Ingredients:

- 1 pound ground pork
- 1 small carrot, grated
- 1 small bell pepper, chopped
- 1 cup tortilla chips, crushed
- 1 small shallot, chopped
- 1 teaspoon garlic, minced
- 1 egg, whisked

Directions:

1. Select the “Air Fry” function and adjust the temperature to 390 degrees F and the time to 25 minutes. Press the “Start” key.
2. Meanwhile, brush silicone muffin cups with nonstick cooking oil. Mix all the ingredients until well combined. Divide the mixture between the muffin cups.
3. When the display indicates “Add Food”, place the muffin cups on the cooking tray.
4. Bake the mini meatloaves in the preheated air fryer oven until cooked through. Bon appétit!

Nutrition:

- Info425 Calories,25.9g Fat,23.7g Carbs,24.2g Protei.

Picnic Shoulder Roast

Servings: 6
Cooking Time: 3 Hours

Ingredients:

- 2 pounds picnic shoulder
- 1 teaspoon garlic, minced
- 1 teaspoon dried rosemary
- 1 teaspoon dried oregano
- Sea salt and ground black pepper

Directions:

1. Pat the ham dry.
2. Select the “Air Fry” function and adjust the temperature to 250 degrees F. Select the “Rotate“ function, and set the time to 3 hours. Press the “Start” key.
3. When the display indicates “Add Food”, place the prepared ham with the rotisserie spit into the oven.
4. Meanwhile, mix all the remaining ingredients to make the glaze. When the ham has reached 145 degrees F, brush the glaze over all surfaces of the ham.
5. Allow it to rest for 10 minutes before slicing and serving.
6. Bon appétit!

Nutrition:

- Info398 Calories,31.2g Fat,3g Carbs,24.6g Protei.

Smoked Paprika Pork Belly

Servings: 5

Cooking Time: 1 Hour

Ingredients:

- 1 pound pork belly
- Sea salt and ground black pepper, to taste
- 1 tablespoon smoked paprika
- 1 teaspoon dried rosemary
- 1 teaspoon dried oregano

Directions:

1. Select the “Air Fry” function and adjust the temperature to 390 degrees F. Press the “Start” key. Place aluminum foil onto the drip pan.
2. Toss the pork with the remaining ingredients.
3. When the display indicates “Add Food”, place the pork in the air fryer oven perforated pan. Cook the pork for about 25 minutes.
4. Decrease the temperature to 360 degrees F. Turn it over and continue to roast for about 30 minutes or until it reaches an internal temperature of 145 degrees F on a meat thermometer.
5. Bon appétit!

Nutrition:

- Info478 Calories,48.3g Fat,1.7g Carbs,8.8g Protei.

Festive Round Roast

Servings: 6

Cooking Time: 50 Minutes

Ingredients:

- 2 ½ pounds round roast
- 1 teaspoon garlic, pressed
- 2 tablespoons olive oil
- 2 tablespoons Cajun seasoning blend

Directions:

1. Select the “Roast” function and adjust the temperature to 360 degrees F. Set the oven to “Rotate” and set the time to 45 minutes. Press the “Start” key.
2. Pat the beef dry. Rub the garlic, olive oil, and Cajun seasoning all over the round roast.
3. When the display indicates “Add Food”, place the beef in the rotisserie basket.
4. Roast the beef until it reaches an internal temperature of 160 degrees F on a meat thermometer.
5. Bon appétit!

Nutrition:

- Info295 Calories,11.5g Fat,1.9g Carbs,42g Protei.

Smoked Paprika Meatballs

Servings: 4
Cooking Time: 20 Minutes

Ingredients:

- 1 ½ pounds ground pork
- 2 tablespoons butter
- Sea salt and ground black pepper, to taste
- 1 small onion, chopped
- 2 garlic cloves, minced
- 1 teaspoon mustard seeds
- 1 teaspoon smoked paprika
- 1/2 teaspoon ground cumin

Directions:

1. Select the "Air Fry" function and adjust the temperature to 380 degrees F. Press the "Start" key.
2. Place a sheet of parchment paper in the air fryer oven pan.
3. In a mixing bowl, thoroughly combine all the ingredients. Then, drop rounds of the mixture in a single layer onto the prepared pan using a small scoop.
4. Air fry the meatballs for 10 minutes.
5. Select the "Broil" function and cook your meatballs for a further 5 minutes or until cooked through.
6. Bon appétit!

Nutrition:

- Info511 Calories,42.1g Fat,3.8g Carbs,29g Protei.

Dijon Pork Chops

Servings: 4
Cooking Time: 20 Minutes

Ingredients:

- 1 ½ pounds pork blade chops
- 4 tablespoons mayonnaise
- 1 tablespoon Dijon mustard
- 1/2 cup seasoned breadcrumbs
- 1 teaspoon garlic powder
- 1/2 onion powder
- Sea salt and ground black pepper, to taste

Directions:

1. Select the "Air Fry" function and adjust the temperature to 400 degrees F. Press the "Start" key. Now, grease the air fryer oven perforated pan with olive oil.
2. Toss the pork chops with the other ingredients.
3. When the display indicates "Add Food", place the pork chops in the air fryer oven perforated pan.
4. Air fry them for 15 minutes or until the internal temperature reaches 145 degrees F on a meat thermometer.
5. Serve warm and enjoy!

Nutrition:

- Info425 Calories,23.9g Fat,13.1g Carbs,40g Protei.

Buttery Tenderloin Filets

Servings: 4
Cooking Time: 20 Minutes

Ingredients:

- 1 pound beef tenderloin filets
- 1/4 cup red wine
- 2 tablespoons soy sauce
- 1 teaspoon mustard seeds
- 2 tablespoons butter, melted
- Sea salt and ground black pepper, to taste
- 1 teaspoon paprika
- 1 teaspoon garlic, minced

Directions:

1. Add all the ingredients to a ceramic or glass bowl. Allow the beef to marinate for at least 3 hours.
2. Select the "Air Fry" function and adjust the temperature to 380 degrees F. Press the "Start" key. Place aluminum foil onto the drip pan.
3. When the display indicates "Add Food", place the beef in the air fryer oven perforated pan. Reserve the marinade. Cook the beef for about 12 minutes.
4. Increase the temperature of the oven to 400 degrees F; baste the beef with the reserved marinade and continue to cook for 5 to 6 minutes more.
5. Serve warm and enjoy!

Nutrition:

- Info367 Calories,28.6g Fat,3.9g Carbs,23.3g Protei.

Flanken-style Beef Ribs

Servings: 4
Cooking Time: 20 Minutes + Marinating Time

Ingredients:

- 1 ½ pounds Flanken-style beef ribs
- 1/4 cup brown sugar
- 1 tablespoon kosher salt
- 1 teaspoon freshly ground black pepper
- 1 tablespoon chili powder
- 1 teaspoon garlic powder
- 1 teaspoon cayenne pepper
- 1 tablespoon brown mustard
- 2 tablespoons butter
- 1/4 cup bourbon
- 1/2 cup tomato sauce

Directions:

1. Add all the ingredients to a ceramic or glass bowl. Allow the beef to marinate for at least 3 hours.
2. Select the "Air Fry" function and adjust the temperature to 360 degrees F. Press the "Start" key. Place aluminum foil onto the drip pan.
3. When the display indicates "Add Food", place the beef ribs in the air fryer oven perforated pan. Reserve the marinade. Cook the beef for about 15 minutes.
4. Serve immediately and enjoy!

Nutrition:

- Info570 Calories,40.5g Fat,15.1g Carbs,33.9g Protei.

Beef Eye Round Roast

Servings: 5
Cooking Time: 50 Minutes
Ingredients:

- 2 pounds beef eye round roast
- 2 tablespoons olive oil
- 2 garlic cloves, pressed
- 1 teaspoon dried basil
- 1 teaspoon dried oregano
- 1 teaspoon dried rosemary
- 1 teaspoon red pepper flakes, crushed
- Sea salt and ground black pepper, to taste

Directions:

1. Select the "Roast" function and adjust the temperature to 360 degrees F. Set the oven to "Rotate" and set the time to 45 minutes. Press the "Start" key.
2. Pat the beef dry. Rub olive oil, garlic, and spices all over the round roast.
3. When the display indicates "Add Food", place the beef in the rotisserie basket.
4. Roast the beef until it reaches an internal temperature of 160 degrees F on a meat thermometer.
5. Bon appétit!

Nutrition:

- Info393 Calories,20.9g Fat,0.6g Carbs,48.5g Protei.

Italian-style Pulled Pork

Servings: 5
Cooking Time: 55 Minutes + Marinating Time
Ingredients:

- 2 pounds boneless pork shoulder
- 1 tablespoon Italian seasoning mix
- 1/2 teaspoon cumin seeds
- 2 garlic cloves, pressed
- Sea salt and ground black pepper, to taste
- 1 teaspoon hot paprika

Directions:

1. Add all the ingredients to a ceramic or glass bowl. Allow the pork to marinate for at least 3 hours.
2. Select the "Air Fry" function and adjust the temperature to 360 degrees F. Press the "Start" key. Place aluminum foil onto the drip pan.
3. When the display indicates "Add Food", place the pork in the air fryer oven perforated pan. Reserve the marinade. Cook the pork for about 25 minutes.
4. Baste the pork with the reserved marinade and continue to roast for about 25 minutes or until cooked through. Shred the pork with two forks and serve immediately.
5. Bon appétit!

Nutrition:

- Info346 Calories,22.5g Fat,1.4g Carbs,31.8g Protei.

Garlic Butter Flank Steak

Servings: 4

Cooking Time: 15 Minutes + Marinating Time

Ingredients:

- 1 ½ pounds flank steak
- 1 cup tomato sauce
- 1 tablespoon Dijon mustard
- Sea salt and freshly cracked black pepper, to taste
- 1 teaspoon cayenne pepper
- 1/2 stick butter, at room temperature
- 2 tablespoons fresh parsley, chopped
- 2 tablespoons fresh basil, chopped
- 2 tablespoons fresh chives, chopped
- 2 garlic cloves, minced

Directions:

1. Add the steak, tomato sauce, and mustard to a ceramic or glass bowl. Allow the beef to marinate for at least 2 hours.
2. Select the "Air Fry" function and adjust the temperature to 400 degrees F. Press the "Start" key. Place aluminum foil onto the drip pan.
3. When the display indicates "Add Food", place the steak in the air fryer oven perforated pan. Cook the steak for about 10 minutes turning it twice during the cooking time.
4. Mix the remaining ingredients and spread the mixture all over your steak. Select the "Broil" function and continue cooking for 4 minutes more.
5. Serve warm and enjoy!

Nutrition:

- Info417 Calories,20.5g Fat,15.7g Carbs,38.9g Protei.

Smoked Sausage With Cauliflower

Servings: 5

Cooking Time: 15 Minutes

Ingredients:

- 1 pound smoked sausages
- 1 pound cauliflower florets
- 2 tablespoons soy sauce
- 1 teaspoon Italian seasoning blend
- Sea salt and ground black pepper, to taste

Directions:

1. Select the "Air Fry" function and adjust the temperature to 400 degrees F. Press the "Start" key. Place aluminum foil onto the drip pan.
2. Toss all the ingredients in a mixing bowl.
3. When the display indicates "Add Food", place the sausage and cauliflower in the air fryer oven perforated pan. Cook the sausage and cauliflower for about 5 minutes.
4. Turn them over and continue to cook for a further 5 minutes.
5. Bon appétit!

Nutrition:

- Info369 Calories,26.2g Fat,11.1g Carbs,19.7g Protei.

Restaurant-style Hamburgers

Servings: 4
Cooking Time: 30 Minutes

Ingredients:

- 1 pound ground chuck
- Kosher salt and ground black pepper, to taste
- 1 teaspoon cayenne pepper
- 1 small onion, chopped
- 2 garlic cloves, minced
- 1 chili pepper, minced
- 4 hamburger buns
- 8 lettuce leaves
- 2 teaspoons yellow mustard
- 4 teaspoons mayonnaise

Directions:

1. Select the “Air Fry” function and adjust the temperature to 390 degrees F. Press the “Start” key.
2. Place a sheet of parchment paper in the air fryer oven pan.
3. Mix the ground chuck, salt, black pepper, cayenne pepper, onion, garlic, and chili pepper until well combined.
4. Shape the mixture into four patties and place them in a single layer in the air fryer oven perforated pan.
5. Air fry your hamburgers for 25 minutes. Assemble your hamburgers with warm patties, hamburger buns, lettuce, mustard, and mayo.
6. Bon appétit!

Nutrition:

- Info375 Calories,17.8g Fat,25.8g Carbs,27.3g Protei.

Roast Pork With Crackling

Servings: 4
Cooking Time: 1 Hour

Ingredients:

- 1 ½ pounds pork butt, skin on
- 1 tablespoon olive oil
- Sea salt and ground black pepper, to taste
- 1 teaspoon smoked paprika
- 1 teaspoon mustard powder
- 1 teaspoon garlic powder

Directions:

1. Using the rotisserie spit, push through the pork butt and attach the rotisserie forks.
2. Select the “Roast” function and adjust the temperature to 380 degrees F. Set the oven to “Rotate” and set time to 50 minutes. Press the “Start” key.
3. When the display indicates “Add Food”, place the prepared meat in the oven.
4. Select the “Broil” function and continue cooking for a further 5 minutes. Enjoy!

Nutrition:

- Info494 Calories,33.6g Fat,2.1g Carbs,43.1g Protei.

Asian-style Beef Bowl

Servings: 4
Cooking Time: 20 Minutes

Ingredients:

- 1 pound rib-eye steak, cubed
- 1/2 cup dashi (or beef bone stock)
- 4 tablespoons rice vinegar
- 2 tablespoons soy sauce (or Shoyu sauce)
- 1 teaspoon ginger-garlic paste
- 2 tablespoons agave nectar
- 1 teaspoon red pepper flakes, crushed
- Sea salt and ground black pepper, to taste
- 1 pound Chinese cabbage, cut into wedges
- 1 medium shallot, sliced

Directions:

1. Place the steak, dashi, rice vinegar, soy sauce, ginger-garlic paste, agave nectar, red pepper flakes, salt, and black pepper in a ceramic bowl. Cover and allow the beef to marinate for 3 hours.
2. Select the "Air Fry" function and adjust the temperature to 380 degrees F. Press the "Start" key. Place aluminum foil onto the drip pan.
3. When the display indicates "Add Food", place the steak, cabbage, and shallot in the parchment-lined air fryer oven perforated pan.
4. Cook the steak for about 8 minutes, turning it twice during the cooking time. Increase the temperature to 400 degrees F and continue cooking for 8 minutes more.
5. Serve warm and enjoy!

Nutrition:

- Info377 Calories,25.5g Fat,14.8g Carbs,23.3g Protei.

Mom's Herbed Meatballs

Servings: 4
Cooking Time: 20 Minutes

Ingredients:

- 1 pound ground beef
- 3 green onions, chopped
- 2 green garlic stalks, chopped (or garlic cloves)
- 1/4 cup fresh parsley, chopped
- 2 tablespoons fresh basil, chopped
- 1 tablespoon fresh coriander, chopped
- 1 teaspoon Montreal seasoning mix
- 2 eggs lightly beaten
- 1/2 cup seasoned breadcrumbs
- 1 tablespoon Worcestershire sauce
- 1 teaspoon cayenne pepper
- Kosher salt and ground black pepper, to taste

Directions:

1. Select the "Air Fry" function and adjust the temperature to 390 degrees F. Press the "Start" key.
2. Place a sheet of parchment paper in the air fryer oven pan. Thoroughly combine all the ingredients in a mixing bowl.
3. Form the mixture into eight balls and place them in a single layer in the air fryer oven perforated pan.
4. Air fry the meatballs for 18 minutes or until they reach an internal temperature of 165 degrees F on a meat thermometer. Bon appétit!

Nutrition:

- Info327 Calories,16.9g Fat,14.4g Carbs,26.3g Protei.

Rice, Grains And Pastry Recipes

Tejeringos With Spicy Chocolate

Servings: 4
Cooking Time: 15 Minutes
Ingredients:

- 1 can refrigerated biscuits
- 1/2 cup milk chocolate
- 1/2 teaspoon ground cayenne powder
- 1/2 cup pecans, coarsely chopped

Directions:

1. Select the “Air Fry” function and adjust the temperature to 375 degrees F. Press the “Start” key.
2. Spritz the air fryer oven perforated pan with cooking oil. Separate the dough into eight biscuits.
3. Bake in the preheated air fryer for 4 minutes. Flip the donuts and air fry for an additional 4 minutes.
4. Melt the chocolate in your microwave; whisk in the pepper and pecans. Then, cover the donuts with the chocolate mixture by dipping and rolling around.
5. Bon appétit!

Nutrition:

- Info327 Calories,21.8g Fat,32.4g Carbs,10.2g Protei.

Greek Pita Wraps

Servings: 2
Cooking Time: 15 Minutes
Ingredients:

- 2 Greek-style pitas
- 1/2 cup bacon bits
- 1/4 cup hummus
- 1/4 cup tomato sauce
- 1 cup haloumi cheese, crumbled

Directions:

1. Select the “Air Fry” function and adjust the temperature to 390 degrees F. Press the “Start” key.
2. Assemble pita wraps with Greek pitas and the remaining ingredients. Secure your wraps with toothpicks.
3. Bake your wraps for 8 minutes or until lightly browned.
4. Serve immediately!

Nutrition:

- Info285 Calories,11.4g Fat,35.2g Carbs,12.7g Protei.

Middle Eastern Pita Sandwich

Servings: 2

Cooking Time: 10 Minutes

Ingredients:

- 2 large pitas
- 4 tablespoons hummus
- 1 medium tomato, sliced
- 1 small cucumber, sliced
- 1 teaspoon za'atar
- 2 teaspoons olive oil
- 4 tablespoons Greek-style yogurt
- 1 clove garlic, minced
- Sea salt and cayenne pepper, to taste

Directions:

1. Assemble the pita breads with the other ingredients; you can use a toothpick to secure your pitas.
2. Select the "Toast" function and press the "Start" key.
3. When the display indicates "Add Food", place the sandwich on the air fryer tray.
4. Toast the sandwich for about 4 minutes or so. Enjoy!

Nutrition:

- Info298 Calories,8.9g Fat,45.1g Carbs,10.9g Protei.

Italian-style Oatmeal Cheeseburgers

Servings: 4

Cooking Time: 20 Minutes

Ingredients:

- 2 cups quick-cooking oats
- 1 small onion, chopped
- 2 tablespoons olive oil
- 1/2 cup cheddar cheese, shredded
- 2 garlic cloves, minced
- 1 tablespoon Italian seasoning mix
- 1 teaspoon smoked paprika
- Sea salt and ground black pepper, to taste

Directions:

1. Select the "Air Fry" function and adjust the temperature to 400 degrees F. Press the "Start" key.
2. Place a sheet of parchment paper in the air fryer oven pan. Thoroughly combine all the ingredients.
3. Form the mixture into equal patties and place them in a single layer in the air fryer oven perforated pan.
4. Air fry the patties for 15 minutes or until golden brown. Serve hot and enjoy!

Nutrition:

- Info385 Calories,12.4g Fat,56.3g Carbs,13.7g Protei.

Bulgur And Lentil Croquettes

Servings: 4
Cooking Time: 20 Minutes

Ingredients:

- 2 cups bulgur, cooked and rinsed
- 1 cup red lentils, cooked or boiled
- 1/2 cup breadcrumbs
- 1 medium red beet, shredded and diced
- 1 medium onion, roughly chopped
- 2 cloves garlic, minced
- Kosher salt and freshly ground black pepper, to taste
- 1 teaspoon cayenne pepper
- 1 teaspoon thyme, chopped
- 2 tablespoons tahini

Directions:

1. Select the "Air Fry" function and adjust the temperature to 400 degrees F. Press the "Start" key.
2. Place a sheet of parchment paper in the air fryer oven pan. Thoroughly combine all the ingredients.
3. Form the mixture into equal balls and place them in a single layer in the air fryer oven perforated pan.
4. Air fry the croquettes for 15 minutes or until cooked through. Serve hot and enjoy!

Nutrition:

- Info331 Calories,5.6g Fat,56.4g Carbs,16.7g Protei.

Quiche Pastry Cups

Servings: 6
Cooking Time: 15 Minutes

Ingredients:

- 1 can refrigerated crescent rolls
- 2 large eggs
- 1 cup pasta sauce
- 4 ounces cup Gruyere cheese, shredded

Directions:

1. Spritz 6 standard-size muffin cups with nonstick spray.
2. Cut your dough evenly into 6 squares. Press your dough pieces into muffin cups.
3. Thoroughly combine the eggs, pasta sauce, and cheese; divide the mixture between the muffin cups.
4. Bake the pastry cups at 350 degrees F for about 7 minutes. Serve warm and enjoy!

Nutrition:

- Info227 Calories,10.1g Fat,22.9g Carbs,11.1g Protei.

Easy Pepperoni Pizza

Servings: 1
Cooking Time: 15 Minutes

Ingredients:

- 1 pizza crust
- 1/4 cup pizza sauce
- 1 ounce pepperoni, sliced
- 1 small bell pepper, seeded and sliced
- 1 ounce mozzarella cheese, crumbled

Directions:

1. Select the "Air Fry" function and adjust the temperature to 400 degrees F. Press the "Start" key.
2. Stretch the dough on a work surface lightly dusted with flour. Spread with a layer of pizza sauce.
3. Top with pepperoni, bell pepper, and cheese. Place your pizza on the air fryer tray that is previously greased with olive oil.
4. Bake your pizza for 10 minutes. Serve warm and enjoy!

Nutrition:

- Info423 Calories,17.3g Fat,43.2g Carbs,22.1g Protei.

Italian-style Mini Pies

Servings: 4
Cooking Time: 15 Minutes

Ingredients:

- 1 can refrigerated crescent dough
- 1 medium carrot, grated
- 8 ounces button mushrooms, chopped
- 1 teaspoon Italian seasoning mix
- 1 cup marinara sauce

Directions:

1. Spritz 6 standard-size muffin cups with nonstick spray.
2. Cut your dough evenly into 6 squares. Press your dough pieces into muffin cups.
3. Thoroughly combine the carrot, mushroom, seasonings, and marinara sauce; divide the mixture between the muffin cups.
4. Bake your pastry cups at 350 degrees F for about 7 minutes. Serve warm and enjoy!

Nutrition:

- Info209 Calories,3.8g Fat,37.9g Carbs,6.9g Protei.

Scallion Buttermilk Cruller

Servings: 6
Cooking Time: 25 Minutes
Ingredients:

- 2 cups plain flour
- 1 teaspoon baking powder
- 1 teaspoon baking soda
- 1/2 teaspoon kosher salt
- 1 teaspoon brown sugar
- 2 medium eggs, well-beaten
- 1 cup buttermilk
- 1/3 cup butter
- 1/2 cup Colby cheese, shredded
- 2 tablespoons scallions, chopped

Directions:

1. In a mixing bowl, thoroughly combine all dry ingredients. In another bowl, mix all the wet ingredients.
2. Add the wet mixture to the dry mixture; mix until everything is combined well.
3. Spoon the dough into a lightly greased muffin tin.
4. Select the "Air Fry" function and adjust the temperature to 380 degrees F. Press the "Start" key.
5. Air fry your scones for 20 minutes, checking them occasionally to make sure they are not getting too brown on top.
6. Bon appétit!

Nutrition:

- Info324 Calories,15.8g Fat,34.6g Carbs,10.2g Protei.

Herb Millet Patties

Servings: 4
Cooking Time: 20 Minutes
Ingredients:

- 1 ½ cups millet, cooked
- 1 teaspoon baking powder
- 2 eggs, beaten
- 1 medium onion, chopped
- 2 cloves garlic, pressed
- 2 teaspoons olive oil
- 1 teaspoon ground turmeric
- 1 teaspoon ground coriander
- 1 teaspoon ground cumin
- 1 teaspoon smoked paprika
- A pinch of grated nutmeg
- Sea salt and ground black pepper, to taste
- 2 tablespoons fresh basil, roughly chopped
- 2 tablespoons fresh parsley, roughly chopped
- 1 cup tortilla chips, crushed

Directions:

1. Select the "Air Fry" function and adjust the temperature to 390 degrees F. Press the "Start" key.
2. Brush a baking pan with olive oil and set it aside.
3. In a mixing bowl, thoroughly combine all the ingredients. Shape the mixture into equal patties and place them on the prepared baking pan.
4. Cook the patties for about 15 minutes, turning them over halfway through the cooking time. Bon appétit!

Nutrition:

- Info315 Calories,12.5g Fat,42.8g Carbs,8.2g Protei.

Greek-style Quinoa Croquettes

Servings: 4
Cooking Time: 20 Minutes

Ingredients:

- 2 cups quinoa, cooked and rinsed
- 1 large egg
- 2 tablespoons tapioca flour
- 3 tablespoons instant oats
- 1 medium carrot, finely chopped
- 1 medium onion, finely chopped
- 1 bell pepper, chopped
- 2 cloves garlic, pressed
- 2 tablespoons fresh parsley, chopped
- Sea salt and ground black pepper, to taste
- 1 cup feta cheese, crumbled

Directions:

1. Select the "Air Fry" function and adjust the temperature to 400 degrees F. Press the "Start" key.
2. Place a sheet of parchment paper in the air fryer oven pan. Thoroughly combine all the ingredients.
3. Form the mixture into equal balls and place them in a single layer in the air fryer oven perforated pan.
4. Air fry the croquettes for 15 minutes or until golden brown. Serve hot and enjoy!

Nutrition:

- Info285 Calories,11.4g Fat,35.2g Carbs,12.7g Protei.

Cheesy Garlicky Biscuits

Servings: 6
Cooking Time: 25 Minutes

Ingredients:

- 1 cup all-purpose flour
- 1 cup almond flour
- 1 teaspoon baking powder
- 1/2 teaspoon baking soda
- 1 teaspoon honey
- 1/2 teaspoon coarse sea salt
- 1/2 stick butter, melted
- 1 cup milk
- 1 cup Swiss cheese, shredded
- 4 ounces ham, chopped
- 1 teaspoon garlic, minced

Directions:

1. In a mixing bowl, thoroughly combine all the dry ingredients. In another bowl, mix all the wet ingredients.
2. Add the wet mixture to the dry mixture; mix until everything is combined well.
3. Spoon the dough into a lightly greased muffin tin.
4. Select the "Air Fry" function and adjust the temperature to 380 degrees F. Press the "Start" key.
5. Air fry your scones for 20 minutes, checking them occasionally to make sure they are not getting too brown on top.
6. Bon appétit!

Nutrition:

- Info355 Calories,22.7g Fat,23.3g Carbs,14.9g Protei.

Hot And Spicy Patties

Servings: 4
Cooking Time: 20 Minutes
Ingredients:

- 1 cup chickpeas, cooked or canned
- 1 cup spelt flour
- 1 medium carrot, chopped
- 1 medium onion, chopped
- 2 cloves garlic, minced
- 1 bell pepper, chopped
- 1 teaspoon dried parsley flakes
- 1 teaspoon dried oregano
- 1 teaspoon dried basil
- 1 teaspoon cayenne pepper
- Sea salt and ground black pepper, to taste
- 2 tablespoons flax seeds
- 2 tablespoons sunflower seeds
- 2 tablespoons pumpkin seeds
- 2 teaspoons olive oil

Directions:

1. Select the "Air Fry" function and adjust the temperature to 400 degrees F. Press the "Start" key.
2. Place a sheet of parchment paper in the air fryer oven pan. Thoroughly combine all the ingredients.
3. Form the mixture into equal patties and place them in a single layer in the air fryer oven perforated pan.
4. Air fry the patties for 15 minutes or until golden brown. Serve hot and enjoy!

Nutrition:

- Info299 Calories,10.8g Fat,43.4g Carbs,10.2g Protei.

Country-style Apple Oatmeal Fritters

Servings: 5
Cooking Time: 20 Minutes
Ingredients:

- 2 medium apples, peeled, cored and grated
- 1 cup instant oats
- 1/2 cup rice flour
- 1 teaspoon baking powder
- 1/2 teaspoon baking soda
- 1/2 cup brown sugar
- 2 medium eggs, whisked
- 2 tablespoons olive oil
- 1 teaspoon ground cinnamon
- A pinch of grated nutmeg
- A pinch of kosher salt

Directions:

1. Select the "Air Fry" function and adjust the temperature to 400 degrees F. Press the "Start" key.
2. Place a sheet of parchment paper in the air fryer oven pan. Thoroughly combine all the ingredients.
3. Air fry your fritters for 15 minutes or until golden brown and cooked through.
4. Bon appétit!

Nutrition:

- Info330 Calories,9.6g Fat,53.9g Carbs,8.7g Protei.

Greek-style Pastry

Servings: 6

Cooking Time: 25 Minutes

Ingredients:

- 2 cups flour
- 1 teaspoon baking powder
- 1/2 teaspoon baking soda
- 1/2 kosher salt
- 1/2 cup Greek yogurt
- 1 large egg
- 1/4 cup honey
- 1/2 cup butter, at room temperature
- 2 ounces walnuts, coarsely chopped

Directions:

1. In a mixing bowl, thoroughly combine all the dry ingredients. In another bowl, mix all the wet ingredients.
2. Add the wet mixture to the dry mixture; fold in the walnuts and mix until everything is combined well.
3. Spoon the dough into a lightly greased muffin tin.
4. Select the "Air Fry" function and adjust the temperature to 380 degrees F. Press the "Start" key.
5. Air fry your scones for 20 minutes, checking them occasionally to make sure they are not getting too brown on top.
6. Bon appétit!

Nutrition:

- Info416 Calories,23.3g Fat,45.7g Carbs,7.7g Protei.

Classic Coconut Cereal

Servings: 10

Cooking Time: 45 Minutes

Ingredients:

- 2 cups instant oats
- 1/2 cup unsalted almonds
- 1/2 cup unsalted cashews
- 1/2 cup honey
- 1/4 cup peanut oil
- A pinch of sea salt
- 1/4 cup almond butter
- 1/4 cup chia seeds
- 1/2 cup coconut flakes

Directions:

1. Select the "Air Fry" function and adjust the temperature to 260 degrees F. Press the "Start" key.
2. Thoroughly combine all ingredients and spread the mixture onto the parchment-lined air fryer tray.
3. Bake your granola for 40 minutes, rotating the pan once or twice during cooking.
4. This granola can be kept in an airtight container for up to 2 weeks. Bon appétit!

Nutrition:

- Info392 Calories,22.2g Fat,42.5g Carbs,9.2g Protei.

Mediterranean Lavash Wraps

Servings: 4
Cooking Time: 15 Minutes

Ingredients:

- 2 lavash (flatbread)
- 1/4 cup tomato ketchup
- 1/2 cup hummus
- 1/4 cup Kalamata black olives, pitted and sliced
- 1 teaspoon Dijon mustard

Directions:

1. Select the "Air Fry" function and adjust the temperature to 390 degrees F. Press the "Start" key.
2. Assemble the Mediterranean wraps with lavash and the remaining ingredients. Secure your wraps with toothpicks.
3. Bake your Mediterranean wraps for 8 minutes or until lightly browned.
4. Serve immediately!

Nutrition:

- Info297 Calories,6.2g Fat,46.6g Carbs,8.7g Protei.

Barley Vegetable Fritters

Servings: 4
Cooking Time: 20 Minutes

Ingredients:

- 2 cups barley, cooked
- 1 medium stalk celery, chopped
- 1 medium carrot, finely chopped
- 2 garlic cloves, minced
- 2 scallion stalks, chopped
- Sea salt and ground black pepper, to taste
- 1 teaspoon dried parsley
- 1 teaspoon dried oregano
- 1 teaspoon dried basil
- 1 cup seasoned breadcrumbs
- 2 tablespoons olive oil

Directions:

1. Select the "Air Fry" function and adjust the temperature to 400 degrees F. Press the "Start" key.
2. Place a sheet of parchment paper in the air fryer oven pan. Thoroughly combine all the ingredients.
3. Form the mixture into equal balls and place them in a single layer in the air fryer oven perforated pan.
4. Air fry the fritters for 15 minutes or until golden brown. Serve hot and enjoy!

Nutrition:

- Info218 Calories,7.7g Fat,34.1g Carbs,5.2g Protei.

Classic Buckwheat Pancakes

Servings: 4
Cooking Time: 20 Minutes
Ingredients:

- 5 tablespoons plain flour
- 5 tablespoons buckwheat flour
- 1 teaspoon baking powder
- A pinch of kosher salt
- A pinch of grated nutmeg
- 1 large egg
- 1/2 cup plain milk
- 2 teaspoons olive oil

Directions:

1. In a mixing bowl, thoroughly combine the dry ingredients. In another bowl, whisk the wet ingredients. Add the wet mixture to the dry ingredients, and mix to combine well.
2. Grease a baking pan with nonstick cooking oil and set it aside.
3. Select the "Air Fry" function and adjust the temperature to 350 degrees F. Press the "Start" key.
4. Cook your pancakes for about 15 minutes, working in batches, if needed. Enjoy!

Nutrition:

- Info123 Calories,4.8g Fat,15.6g Carbs,4.8g Protei.

Rice And Bacon Croquettes

Servings: 5
Cooking Time: 15 Minutes
Ingredients:

- 2 cups white rice, cooked
- 3 ounces smoked bacon, chopped
- 1 cup mozzarella cheese, shredded
- 1 cup Italian breadcrumb
- 2 eggs
- 2 teaspoons olive oil

Directions:

1. Select the "Air Fry" function and adjust the temperature to 400 degrees F. Press the "Start" key.
2. Place a sheet of parchment paper in the air fryer oven pan. Thoroughly combine all the ingredients.
3. Form the mixture into equal balls and place them in a single layer in the air fryer oven perforated pan.
4. Air fry the croquettes for 11 minutes or until golden brown. Serve hot and enjoy!

Nutrition:

- Info325 Calories,21.4g Fat,27.6g Carbs,20.2g Protei.

Desserts Recipes

Candied Honey Pecans

Servings: 8

Cooking Time: 15 Minutes

Ingredients:

- 1/2 pound pecan halves
- 1 egg white
- 1 tablespoon fresh orange juice
- 2 tablespoons brown sugar
- 1/2 cup honey
- 1 teaspoon ground cinnamon
- A pinch of grated nutmeg
- A pinch of coarse sea salt

Directions:

1. Select the "Roast" function and adjust the temperature to 320 degrees F. Press the "Start" key.
2. In a mixing dish, toss all the ingredients.
3. When the display indicates "Add Food", place the almonds in the air fryer oven pan.
4. Roast your pecans in the preheated air fryer for 8 minutes, tossing them halfway through the cooking time to ensure even cooking.
5. Bon appétit!

Nutrition:

- Info277 Calories,20.3g Fat,25g Carbs,3.2g Protei.

Cinnamon Waffle Sticks

Servings: 4

Cooking Time: 15 Minutes

Ingredients:

- 4 frozen waffles, cut into thirds
- 4 teaspoons butter, softened
- 1 tablespoon cinnamon powder
- 2 tablespoons agave syrup

Directions:

1. Select the "Air Fry" function and adjust the temperature to 350 degrees F. Press the "Start" key.
2. Air fry the waffles for about 3 minutes. Flip the waffles and continue to cook for 3 minutes.
3. Toss the waffle sticks with the butter, cinnamon, and agave syrup and serve immediately. Enjoy!

Nutrition:

- Info188 Calories,7.9g Fat,17.4g Carbs,2.3g Protei.

Decadent Chocolate Croissants

Servings: 4
Cooking Time: 20 Minutes
Ingredients:

- 1 can refrigerated crescent rolls
- 2 tablespoons almond butter (or peanut butter)
- 3 ounces hazelnuts, finely chopped
- 1/2 cup chocolate syrup

Directions:

1. Separate the crescent rolls into eight triangles. Spread each triangle with almond butter and hazelnuts. Roll them up and lower them into the baking pan.
2. Select the "Air Fry" function and adjust the temperature to 350 degrees F. Press the "Start" key.
3. Air fry your croissants at 340 degrees F for about 15 minutes or until golden brown.
4. Drizzle the warm croissants with chocolate syrup and enjoy!

Nutrition:

- Info484 Calories,29.6g Fat,51.4g Carbs,7.7g Protei.

Almond Energy Bars

Servings: 8
Cooking Time: 35 Minutes
Ingredients:

- 1 cup old-fashioned rolled oats
- 1 cup almond meal
- 1/2 cup brown sugar
- 2 tablespoons honey
- 1 ½ teaspoons baking powder
- 1/4 teaspoon salt
- 1/2 teaspoon ground cinnamon
- 1/2 cup peanut butter
- 1/2 cup almond milk
- 2 eggs
- 1 teaspoon vanilla extract
- 2 ounces dried cranberries

Directions:

1. Select the "Air Fry" function and adjust the temperature to 360 degrees F. Press the "Start" key.
2. In a large mixing bowl, stir together all the dry ingredients. In another bowl, mix the wet ingredients.
3. Add the wet mixture to the dry ingredients and stir to combine well. Fold in the cranberries.
4. Press the batter onto a parchment-lined baking pan. Bake the bars for approximately 15 minutes or until golden brown.
5. Let it sit on a wire rack for 20 minutes before slicing and serving.
6. Bon appétit!

Nutrition:

- Info285 Calories,11.8g Fat,37.1g Carbs,8.8g Protei.

Mom's Famous Flapjacks

Servings: 5
Cooking Time: 20 Minutes
Ingredients:

- 1 cup all-purpose flour
- 1/2 cup besan (chickpea flour)
- 4 tablespoons sugar
- 1 teaspoon baking powder
- Kosher salt and freshly grated nutmeg, to taste
- 2 tablespoons butter, softened
- 2 large eggs, room temperature
- 1 cup coconut milk
- 1 teaspoon vanilla extract

Directions:

1. In a mixing bowl, thoroughly combine the dry ingredients. In another bowl, whisk the wet ingredients. Add the wet mixture to dry ingredients, and mix to combine well.
2. Grease a baking pan with nonstick cooking oil and set it aside.
3. Select the "Air Fry" function and adjust the temperature to 350 degrees F. Press the "Start" key.
4. Cook your flapjacks for about 13 minutes, working in batches, if needed. Enjoy!

Nutrition:

- Info254 Calories,8.9g Fat,33.3g Carbs,8.7g Protei.

Authentic Cuban Tostada

Servings: 2
Cooking Time: 15 Minutes
Ingredients:

- 2 teaspoons butter
- 2 large eggs
- 2 tablespoons coconut milk
- 1/2 teaspoon vanilla extract
- 1/2 teaspoon ground cinnamon
- 1/3 cup brown sugar
- 4 slices thick white bread

Directions:

1. Select the "air fryer" function and adjust the temperature to 390 degrees F. Press the "Start" key.
2. In a mixing dish, whisk the butter, eggs, coconut milk, vanilla, cinnamon, and sugar.
3. Dip all the slices of bread in this mixture.
4. When the display indicates "Add Food", place the French toast in the air fryer oven pan.
5. Bake in the preheated air fryer for 10 minutes, turning them over halfway through the cooking time to ensure even cooking.
6. Enjoy!

Nutrition:

- Info338 Calories,10.9g Fat,46.4g Carbs,13.1g Protei.

Classic French Toast With Honey

Servings: 4
Cooking Time: 15 Minutes

Ingredients:

- 2 eggs, beaten
- 2 tablespoons half-and-half
- 1/2 teaspoons ground cinnamon
- 1/4 teaspoons ground cardamom
- 1/2 teaspoon vanilla extract
- 1 loaf challah bread, cut into thick slices
- 4 tablespoons honey

Directions:

1. Select the "air fryer" function and adjust the temperature to 390 degrees F. Press the "Start" key.
2. In a mixing dish, whisk the eggs, half-and-half, cinnamon, cardamom, and vanilla extract.
3. Dip all the slices of challah bread in this mixture.
4. When the display indicates "Add Food", place the French toast in the air fryer oven pan.
5. Bake in the preheated air fryer for 10 minutes, turning them over halfway through the cooking time to ensure even cooking.
6. Drizzle your French toast with honey and enjoy!

Nutrition:

- Info412 Calories,6.2g Fat,75.2g Carbs,13.1g Protei.

Favorite Chocolate Lava Cake

Servings: 4
Cooking Time: 15 Minutes

Ingredients:

- 2 large eggs
- 1/2 stick butter, softened
- 4 ounces dark chocolate chunks
- 1/2 cup brown sugar
- A pinch of kosher salt
- A pinch of grated nutmeg
- 1/2 teaspoon ground cinnamon
- 2 tablespoons cocoa powder
- 4 tablespoons almond flour

Directions:

1. Select the "Air Fry" function and adjust the temperature to 375 degrees F. Press the "Start" key.
2. Brush four ramekins with nonstick spray.
3. Whisk the eggs with sugar until frothy. Add in the remaining ingredients and mix to combine.
4. Spoon the batter into the prepared ramekins and bake your lava cake for 10 minutes. Serve warm.

Nutrition:

- Info446 Calories,31.3g Fat,34.9g Carbs,8.1g Protei.

Fluffy Almond Brownie Squares

Servings: 6
Cooking Time: 20 Minutes
Ingredients:

- 1/4 cup all-purpose flour
- 1/4 cup almond meal
- 2/3 cup granulated sugar
- 1/2 cup cocoa powder
- 1/2 teaspoon baking powder
- A pinch of kosher salt
- A pinch of grated nutmeg
- 1/3 cup coconut oil, melted
- 2 eggs, beaten

Directions:

1. Brush a baking pan with nonstick cooking spray oil; set it aside.
2. Mix the dry ingredients in a bowl; now, thoroughly combine the wet ingredients. Add the wet mixture to the dry mixture and mix until everything is well incorporated.
3. Select the "Bake" function and adjust the temperature to 330 degrees F. Press the "Start" key. When the display indicates "Add Food", place the baking pan on the air fryer tray.
4. Bake your brownie for 15 minutes or until a tester comes out clean when inserted in the middle.
5. Bon appétit!

Nutrition:

- Info277 Calories,16.3g Fat,33.2g Carbs,4.5g Protei.

Maple Toast Sticks

Servings: 3
Cooking Time: 15 Minutes
Ingredients:

- 2 large eggs
- 1/4 cup milk
- 2 tablespoons half-and-half
- 2 tablespoons butter, melted
- 1 teaspoon vanilla extract
- 1 teaspoon ground cinnamon
- 6 slices day-old bread, cut into sticks
- 2 tablespoons maple syrup

Directions:

1. Select the "air fryer" function and adjust the temperature to 390 degrees F. Press the "Start" key.
2. In a mixing dish, whisk the eggs, milk, half-and-half, butter, vanilla, and cinnamon.
3. Dip all the sticks of bread in this mixture.
4. When the display indicates "Add Food", place the French toast in the air fryer oven pan.
5. Bake in the preheated air fryer for 10 minutes, turning them over halfway through the cooking time to ensure even cooking.
6. Drizzle the French toast with maple syrup and enjoy!

Nutrition:

- Info282 Calories,13g Fat,31.7g Carbs,8.7g Protei.

Pistachio-stuffed Apricots

Servings: 3
Cooking Time: 15 Minutes

Ingredients:

- 1/2 cup mascarpone cheese, at room temperature
- 1/4 cup honey
- 1/4 cup pistachios, shelled and finely chopped
- 9 apricots, pitted and halved

Directions:

1. In a mixing bowl, thoroughly combine the mascarpone cheese, honey, and pistachios. Divide the mixture between the apricot halves.
2. Select the "Air Fry" function and adjust the temperature to 350 degrees F. Press the "Start" key.
3. Bake the apricots for 10 to 11 minutes or until tender and lightly caramelized.
4. Serve at room temperature and enjoy!

Nutrition:

- Info228 Calories,6.5g Fat,38.7g Carbs,7.5g Protei.

Classic Cinnamon Tostada

Servings: 2
Cooking Time: 10 Minutes

Ingredients:

- 2 whole-wheat tortillas, cut into triangles
- 2 tablespoons brown sugar
- 1 teaspoon ground cinnamon
- 2 tablespoons butter, softened

Directions:

1. Select the "air fryer" function and adjust the temperature to 390 degrees F. Press the "Start" key.
2. Toss the tortilla chunks with the remaining ingredients.
3. When the display indicates "Add Food", place the French toast in the air fryer oven pan.
4. Bake in the preheated air fryer for 8 minutes, turning them over halfway through the cooking time to ensure even cooking.
5. Enjoy!

Nutrition:

- Info296 Calories,14.3g Fat,38.5g Carbs,4g Protei.

Sweet Cinnamon Almonds

Servings: 6
Cooking Time: 10 Minutes

Ingredients:

- 1 ½ cups raw almonds
- 2 tablespoons salted butter, melted
- 2 tablespoons brown sugar
- 1/2 teaspoon ground cinnamon

Directions:

1. Select the "Roast" function and adjust the temperature to 320 degrees F. Press the "Start" key.
2. In a mixing dish, toss all the ingredients.
3. When the display indicates "Add Food", place the almonds in the air fryer oven pan.
4. Roast your almonds in the preheated air fryer for 8 minutes, tossing them halfway through the cooking time to ensure even cooking.
5. Bon appétit!

Nutrition:

- Info242 Calories,20.4g Fat,10.5g Carbs,7.7g Protei.

Fried Banana Slices

Servings: 1
Cooking Time: 20 Minutes

Ingredients:

- 1 large banana, peeled and sliced
- 1 tablespoon peanut oil
- 1 teaspoon ground cinnamon
- 1/2 teaspoon ground cardamom

Directions:

1. Select the "Air Fry" function and adjust the temperature to 350 degrees F. Press the "Start" key.
2. Toss the banana slices with the remaining ingredients. Bake the banana slices for 5 minutes. Then toss them and continue to cook for 3 minutes longer.
3. Bon appétit!

Nutrition:

- Info251 Calories,14g Fat,33.8g Carbs,1.7g Protei.

Easy Vanilla Donuts

Servings: 8

Cooking Time: 20 Minutes

Ingredients:

- 1 package refrigerated buttermilk biscuits
- 2 tablespoons butter, melted
- Vanilla glaze:
- 1 cup powdered sugar
- 2 ounces coconut milk
- 1 teaspoon pure vanilla extract

Directions:

1. Separate the biscuits and cut holes out of the center of each biscuit using a 1-inch round biscuit cutter; place them on parchment paper. Brush them with melted butter.
2. Select the "Air Fry" function and adjust the temperature to 350 degrees F. Press the "Start" key.
3. Lower your biscuits into the baking pan.
4. Air fry your biscuits at 340 degrees F for about 15 minutes or until golden brown, flipping them halfway through the cooking time.
5. Meanwhile, in a medium bowl, whisk together the powdered sugar, milk, and vanilla until smooth and creamy.
6. Dip the warm donuts into the vanilla glaze and enjoy!

Nutrition:

- Info222 Calories,8.4g Fat,31.7g Carbs,2.4g Protei.

Greek-style Banana Cake

Servings: 6

Cooking Time: 20 Minutes

Ingredients:

- 3/4 cup cake flour
- 3/4 cup caster sugar
- 1/2 cup butter, melted
- 2 medium eggs, beaten
- 1/2 teaspoon almond extract
- 1/2 teaspoon vanilla extract
- 1/4 teaspoon ground cardamom
- 1/3 teaspoon crystallized ginger
- 1/4 cup Greek-style yogurt
- 2 overripe bananas, peeled and mashed

Directions:

1. Brush a baking pan with a nonstick cooking spray oil; set it aside.
2. Mix the dry ingredients; thoroughly combine the wet ingredients. Add the wet mixture to the dry mixture and mix until everything is well incorporated.
3. Select the "Bake" function and adjust the temperature to 330 degrees F. Press the "Start" key. When the display indicates "Add Food", place the baking pan on the air fryer tray.
4. Bake banana bread for 15 minutes or until a tester comes out clean when inserted in the middle.
5. Bon appétit!

Nutrition:

- Info359 Calories,17.1g Fat,48.4g Carbs,4.8g Protei.

Baked Plums With Almond Topping

Servings: 4
Cooking Time: 15 Minutes
Ingredients:

- 8 fresh plums, pitted and halved
- 2 teaspoons coconut oil
- 8 teaspoons ground almonds
- 8 teaspoons coconut sugar

Directions:

1. Top the plum halves with the remaining ingredients.
2. Select the "Air Fry" function and adjust the temperature to 350 degrees F. Press the "Start" key.
3. Bake the plum halves for 10 minutes or until tender and lightly caramelized.
4. Serve at room temperature and enjoy!

Nutrition:

- Info136 Calories,5.6g Fat,21.3g Carbs,2.2g Protei.

Golden Banana Bites

Servings: 3
Cooking Time: 15 Minutes
Ingredients:

- 1 large egg, beaten
- 1/2 cup rice flour
- 1/2 cup breadcrumbs
- 1/2 teaspoon ground cinnamon
- 1/4 teaspoon grated nutmeg
- 1/4 teaspoon ground cloves
- 2 tablespoons coconut sugar
- 2 medium bananas, peeled and sliced

Directions:

1. Select the "Air Fry" function and adjust the temperature to 350 degrees F. Press the "Start" key.
2. In a mixing dish, thoroughly combine the egg and rice flour. In a separate bowl, mix the remaining ingredients until well combined.
3. Dredge each slice of banana into the flour mixture. Then, roll them over the breadcrumb mixture.
4. Bake the banana slices in the preheated air fryer for approximately 10 minutes, flipping them halfway through the cooking time. Bon appétit!

Nutrition:

- Info234 Calories,2.6g Fat,48.4g Carbs,50.2g Protei.

Old-fashioned Walnut Brownies

Servings: 6
Cooking Time: 20 Minutes

Ingredients:

- 1/2 cup flour
- 2 tablespoons walnuts, chopped
- 1 teaspoon baking powder
- 1/2 cup butter, melted
- 1 cup brown sugar
- 1 teaspoon vanilla extract
- 2 eggs
- 1/2 cup cocoa powder

Directions:

1. Brush a baking pan with a nonstick cooking spray oil; set it aside.
2. Mix dry ingredients, then, thoroughly combine the wet ingredients. Add the wet mixture to the dry mixture and mix until everything is well incorporated.
3. Select the "Bake" function and adjust the temperature to 330 degrees F. Press the "Start" key. When the display indicates "Add Food", place the baking pan on the air fryer tray.
4. Bake your brownie for 15 minutes or until a tester comes out clean when inserted in the middle.
5. Bon appétit!

Nutrition:

- Info303 Calories,19.3g Fat,29.2g Carbs,5g Protei.

Apple Almond Crisp

Servings: 8

Cooking Time: 20 Minutes

Ingredients:

- 2 large apples, peeled, cored and diced
- 1/2 teaspoon ground cardamom
- 1/2 teaspoon ground cinnamon
- 1/4 teaspoon ground nutmeg
- 2 tablespoons almonds, slivered
- Topping:
- 1/2 cup all-purpose flour
- 1/2 cup almond meal
- 1/2 teaspoon baking powder
- 1/4 teaspoon sea salt
- 1/2 cup brown sugar
- 2 eggs, beaten
- 1/2 cup coconut oil

Directions:

1. Select the "Air Fry" function and adjust the temperature to 360 degrees F. Press the "Start" key.
2. Toss the apples with cardamom, cinnamon, nutmeg, and almonds in a lightly greased baking pan.
3. Mix the flour, almond meal, baking powder, salt, and sugar in a bowl. Then, stir in the eggs and coconut oil. Mix until smooth and uniform.
4. Drop tablespoons of the batter onto the fruit layer. Lower the pan onto the air fryer tray and bake your crisp for approximately 12 minutes or until the apples are bubbly and the topping is golden brown.
5. Bon appétit!

Nutrition:

- Info258 Calories,18.4g Fat,21.7g Carbs,3.8g Protei.

RECIPES INDEX